One, Two, Three . . . Echo Me!

Ready-to-Use Songs, Games, and Activities to Help Children Sing in Tune

Loretta Mitchell

HERITAGE MUSIC PRESS

A DIVISION OF THE LORENZ CORPORATION
Box 802 / Dayton, OH 45401-0802 / www.lorenz.com

Previously published
© 1991 by Parker Publishing Company, Inc.
a division of Prentice Hall, Inc.
West Nyack, New York

10 9 8 7 6 5 4

Library of Congress Cataloging-in-Publication Data

Mitchell, Loretta, 1951–
    One, two, three—echo me!

    A collection of original songs, games, and
activities designed to teach children to match pitches
and sing in tune.
    1. Children's songs. 2. Singing games. 3. Singing—
Instruction and study—Juvenile. [1. Songs. 2. Singing—
Instruction and study] I. Title.
M1994.M6805 1991   90-751610
ISBN 0-89328-157-3

ISBN 0-89328-157-3

HERITAGE MUSIC PRESS
A DIVISION OF THE LORENZ CORPORATION
Box 802 / Dayton, OH 45401-0802 / www.lorenz.com

Printed in the United States of America

About the Author

Loretta Mitchell teaches elementary general and choral music for the Brainerd (Minnesota) Public Schools. She also serves as the school district's K–12 Music Coordinator. She has taught vocal, instrumental, and general music since 1973. A Phi Beta Kappa, Summa Cum Laude graduate of St. Olaf College, she toured with both the St. Olaf Band and the St. Olaf Choir. Awarded a graduate fellowship, she received a Master of Science degree in Music Education from the University of Illinois at Urbana–Champaign.

Mrs. Mitchell has been selected Brainerd Teacher of the Year, Minnesota Teacher of Excellence, Minnesota Honor Roll Teacher, and Minnesota Classroom Music Educator of the Year. She has presented workshops and clinics for state music education conferences, administrators, and classroom teachers across the upper midwest. She has held the offices of vice-president and president of Minnesota Elementary Music Educators K–8, as well as classroom music vice-president of Minnesota Music Educators Association. She has served on the Commissioner's Task Force for Restructuring Education, the Minnesota Department of Education Elementary Curriculum Rules Change Committee, and the Minnesota Model Learner Outcome Committee.

Mrs. Mitchell's other publications include *Music Reading Made Simple, Volumes I, II and III* (Mitchell Music Co., 1979, 1981, 1983), *101 Bulletin Boards for the Music Classroom* (Jensen Publications, 1990), and the *Ready-to-Use Music Reading Activities Kit*, Parker Publishing Co., 1991. She is a contributing author to several publications including *The Primary Teacher's Ready-to-Use Activities Program*, published by The Center for Applied Research in Education, a subsidiary of Prentice Hall.

About This Book

One, Two, Three . . . Echo Me! is the vehicle through which countless children have developed the ability to sing in tune. Music specialists and classroom teachers alike may use this collection to help nonsingers become singers and to help singers become more accurate. The songs, games, and activities provide valuable practice in accurate singing, a cornerstone of music learning.

Singing in tune is a learned skill. Children can be taught to imitate pitches and pitch patterns. To develop this skill, children must have repeated opportunities to hear pitch patterns. They must understand the meaning, feeling, and sound of pitch matching. In addition, they need guided practice—matching patterns, hearing their own voices, and assessing their own progress. *One, Two, Three . . . Echo Me!* provides exactly these opportunities with emphasis on echo singing, solo singing, call and response singing, and small group singing.

Elementary students show a wide range of pitch-matching abilities, from the student who has not yet learned to coordinate ear and voice, to the highly confident solo performer. *One, Two, Three . . . Echo Me!* includes exercises for all abilities, encouraging initial success for beginners and extending skills for more advanced students.

Special features of this book include

- a section of activities to help children differentiate between singing and speaking voices;
- special songs and games specifically designed for the older elementary student;
- special songs and games for holiday seasons;
- cross-curricular ideas and strategies that reinforce math, social studies, and language arts skills;
- reproducible masters to simplify teacher preparation;
- extensive teaching suggestions and ideas with each song;
- improvisation activities that encourage student creativity;
- extensive indexing by classification, title, and pitch content of songs.

Through the purposeful games in *One, Two, Three . . . Echo Me!* children improve their singing skills in a positive atmosphere. You create that atmosphere by helping each child build an "I can do it!" attitude. Every child needs to experience success. From an initial success comes self-confidence, more success, and, gradually, the ability to sing in tune.

Loretta Mitchell

General Guidelines and Suggestions for Using This Book

Method for Presenting Songs

Many songs in this collection are short and will require little initial teaching. Longer songs may be presented using the following procedure:

1. Let students hear the whole song.
2. Teach the song in sections, working for accuracy of words and melody.
3. Practice with teacher-supplied responses.
4. Allow time for students to prepare responses.
5. Practice with volunteers singing responses.
6. Sing the entire song.
7. Play the game.

Choosing Soloists

The creative teacher already uses many procedures to choose soloists. Some basic ideas follow.

1. Random on-the-spot selection.
   - Randomly signal soloists as the class sings.
   - Use a card pack. The teacher uses this pack for random selection. Each child writes his or her name on a blank card.
   - Have one soloist choose the next soloist.
   - Pass an item around the classroom. (See the "It's your turn!" disk master 2–4 on page 40.) The student holding the item at the time of the solo is the designated soloist.
   - Go around the room. Each child receives a turn, as long as time permits.
   - Use selection processes specific to each game.

2. Planned selection—plan which students you want to sing specific solos. In this way, you carefully challenge selected children, while actively involving other students.

   ● Signal soloists while the class sings.

   ● Use a card pack. Each child writes his or her name on a blank card. Prior to the class period, you pull cards from the pack, targeting students who need special practice.

   ● Use a class list, record book, or data base. Keep records of each child's progress in matching pitches, and use this information to determine who will sing specific solos.

   ● Go around the room. Each child receives a turn using a teacher-determined starting point. Target specific students for practice on specific skills.

   ● Use selection processes specific to each game, but under your control.

Reinforcing Musical Concepts

These songs and games may be used to teach and review basic musical concepts. Rhythm concepts can be reinforced through such activities as clapping the beat or tapping the melodic rhythm. For added practice with concepts of melodic direction and melodic contour, incorporate the following while working with these songs:

1. Curwen hand signs;
2. body movement to reinforce melodic movement;
3. iconic notation of melodic content;
4. traditional notation of melodic content.

Feedback and Reinforcement

Feedback and reinforcement are vital to accurate singing. Verbal or nonverbal communication from a teacher lets a student know immediately that he or she has done well. The following motivators and reinforcers (some extrinsic, some intrinsic) are helpful as well:

1. praise
2. handshakes
3. notes or phone calls to parents
4. visits to the principal with "good news" notes
5. badges or stickers
6. honor rolls

7. hugs
8. applause
9. displays of students' pictures
10. prizes

Review of Songs

Use these songs and games repeatedly. The full benefit of each activity will appear when students feel confident enough to try new solos, new sounds, and new improvisations.

     Feel free to adapt and create your own variations. Solicit student ideas and contributions. These games can become part of your students' repertoire. Use them year after year for teaching music concepts and skills.

Suggested Grade Levels

Songs, games, and activities in *One, Two, Three ... Echo Me!* list suggested grade levels for use. These grade levels are general guidelines. Feel free to use songs in any grade levels as they seem appropriate. Many songs include suggestions for simplification or extension.

Leader Parts

You will usually sing the leader parts, but you can delegate that role. Many leader parts can be effectively performed by a student.

Improvisation

Encourage students to use creativity with these songs and games. Several exercises include specific suggestions for improvised musical answers.

Student Responses

Sample responses appear throughout the collection in parentheses. Many student answers will require alteration of the notated rhythms.

Masters

Black-line masters are included for many songs in *One, Two, Three ... Echo Me!* The masters provide teaching aids, visual aids, and game pieces. Complete instructions are given for preparation and use of the masters.

A Spirit of Fun and Acceptance

Classroom climate can greatly help a student succeed. Try the following helpful hints:

1. Teach these songs by rote, and play the games as you teach.
2. Keep the classroom atmosphere relaxed.
3. Reinforce any improvement toward better tone matching.
4. Accept any honest attempt by a student. Your attitude will be reflected by the student's peers.
5. Assure students that all of them will learn to sing in tune, and that you want to help each of them become a better singer.
6. Demonstrate accurate listening as a first step in accurate singing.
7. Encourage every student and reinforce the "I can do it!" attitude.

Contents

Indexes • 187

1

Singing/Speaking Voices: Helping the Child Know and Feel the Difference

How can we ask children to sing *in tune,* if we have not taught them how to *sing?* Students discover their singing voices through vocal experimentation. They find various ways to use the voice, exploring the unique feeling, sound, and production of each. The activities in this section enable students to differentiate between singing and speaking, and allow them to experiment with many voices. Through these activities, your students will also improve listening, response, creative thinking, and solo performance skills.

Bake a Cake

Pitch content: Vocal exercise, drmsl

Predominant pitch (es)/pattern(s): sl

Suggested grade level(s): 3 and 4

Formation: Teacher's choice

Materials required:
- "Bake a Cake" speech exercise teacher page (master 1–1)
- "Bake a Cake" optional melody teacher page (master 1–1)
- baking cards (master 1–2)
- optional items cards (master 1–3)

Preparation:
1. Make copies of the baking cards masters. Color them and then laminate for longer wear. Cut the cards apart.
2. Make copies or a transparency of the "Bake a Cake" page.

Procedure:

Distribute the baking cards to several children. Choose a card holder, and name that student in the chant (measure 1). Each card holder names his or her ingredient in a solo (measures 5 through 8). The class responds with Coda A, inserting the name of the soloist and the ingredient.

Other ideas:
1. Distribute the optional cards (items that do not belong in a cake: string, rocks, money, crayons, mittens, etc.) in addition to the ingredient cards. The class, upon hearing each soloist, must decide whether an item belongs in a cake, and respond with Coda A or Coda B.
2. Add a melody. See the suggested melody in master 1–1.
3. Try the game without cards. Instruct students to silently prepare their solos. The leader starts the chant or song by naming any student in the class. The class joins in singing or chanting. The designated student responds with a prepared solo, adding an ingredient to the cake. The class responds with Coda A or Coda B.

Bake a Cake

Bake a Cake

(1–2)

eggs	flour
milk	sugar
butter	flavoring
baking powder	salt

socks

rocks

string

money

bugs

mittens

crayons

stickers

Good King Leopold

Pitch content: msl

Predominant pitch(es)/pattern(s): sm

Suggested grade level(s): preK to 2

Formation: Teacher's choice

Materials required:
- "Good King Leopold" page (master 1–4)
- crown pattern, optional (master 1–5)

Preparation:
1. If crowns are used, make copies of the crown pattern. Color them and then laminate for longer wear. Cut out the crown and cut again along the broken line. Attach the paper strip to the crown front with tape or staples.
2. Make copies or a transparency of the "Good King Leopold" page.

Procedure:

The object of this game is to obtain permission to cross King Leopold's property. Choose one child to be King Leopold, and let him or her wear a crown. The class sings measures 1 through 4. King Leopold answers by singing measures 5 through 8 as a solo. The king chooses which voice to demand of the subjects. For example, if the king sings, "You must ask again. . . ," the class repeats the song using the voice the king has demanded. The repetitions go on at the will of the king. When the king finally says, "YES!" the class members stand and run in place. The king controls how long they run, and makes a large arm gesture to make them sit down. Once they are seated, the game begins again.

Other ideas:
1. Model the king's role several times to help your students understand exactly what you expect.
2. Rehearse whispering, talking, and singing voices before playing the game.
3. Change kings frequently. Give as many children as possible a chance to be the soloist.
4. Let each king keep his or her crown to bring home. Suggest that they teach the game to their brothers and sisters.

Good King Leopold

(1–4)

(1–5)

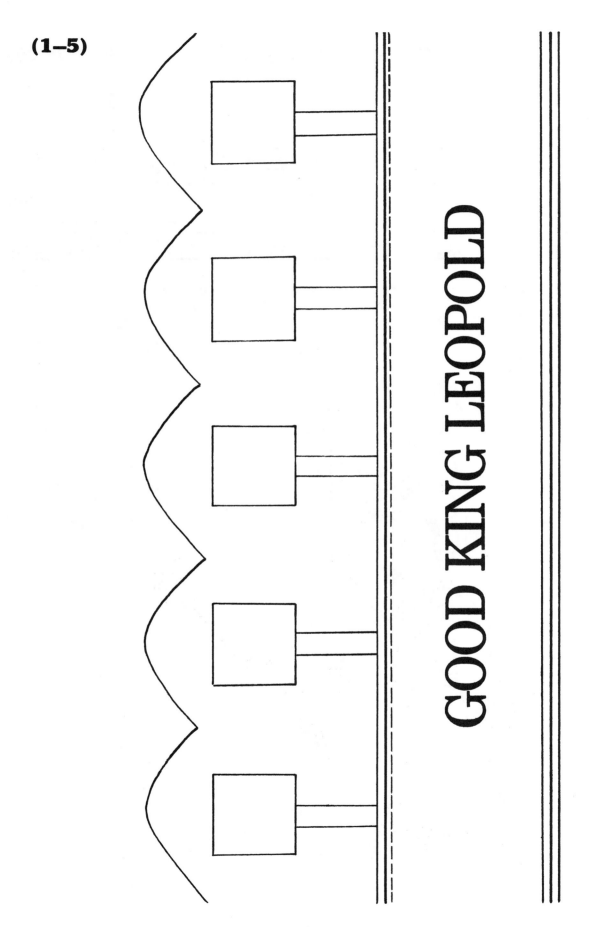

Make a Sound

Pitch content: Vocal exercise, ms

Predominant pitch(es)/pattern(s): sm

Suggested grade level(s): preK to 2

Formation: Circle or classroom formation

Materials required:
- "Make a Sound" page (master 1–6)
- bunny wand patterns (master 1–7)

Preparation:
1. Make copies of the bunny wand patterns. Cut out the front and back circles of the bunny. Color them and then laminate for longer wear. Glue or tape the circles to an unsharpened pencil or a rhythm stick to make a wand.
2. Make copies or a transparency of the "Make a Sound" page.

Procedure:

Take the bunny wand and move around the inside of the circle, tapping each child on the shoulder as the class sings. The child whose shoulder is tapped on the word "smile" is the designated soloist. He or she makes any kind of vocal sound. The class echoes the sound, and starts the song again. The soloist takes the wand and becomes the new leader. The previous leader takes the soloist's place in the circle.

Other ideas:
1. Help your students become comfortable making sounds. Start with easy sounds such as a siren, a cat's "meow," a cow's "moo," the long "eee" sound in various ranges, "buzzz," "zzzziippp," "ah" in various ranges, and "whooo" in various ranges.
2. Help visual learners by illustrating sounds on the chalkboard. Here are a few examples:

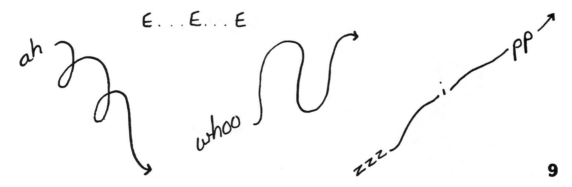

3. Encourage students to explore physical movement while making up sounds. Help them create hand/body motions to match their sounds. Class members should imitate motions as well as sounds.

4. Rehearse several vocal sounds with hand motions before playing this game to help the inhibited child contribute and feel less self conscious.

Make a Sound

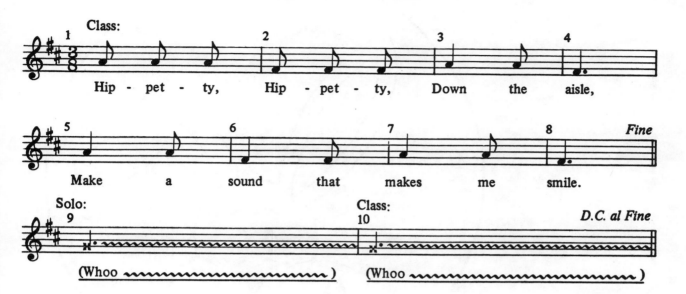

Hip - pet - ty,   Hip - pet - ty,   Down   the   aisle,

Make   a   sound   that   makes   me   smile.

(Whoo ∼∼∼∼∼∼∼∼∼∼∼)   (Whoo ∼∼∼∼∼∼∼∼∼∼∼∼∼∼∼)

(1–7)

"Many Voices" Card Game

Pitch content: Vocal exercise

Suggested grade level(s): 3 to 5

Formation: Small groups

Materials required:

- two decks of cards for each group (masters 1–8 and 1–9)

Preparation:

1. Make copies of master 1–8 on PINK paper. Laminate, if desired, and then cut cards apart. Allow one set of pink cards for each small group.
2. Make copies of master 1–9 on GREEN paper. Laminate, if desired, and then cut cards apart. Allow one set of green cards for each small group.

Procedure:

Teach all students how to play by demonstrating the game with three student volunteers. Divide your class into small groups of three to four members each. Give each group a deck of green cards and a deck of pink cards.

The object of this game is voice experimentation. There is no winner or loser. Shuffle the pink word cards and the green voice cards. Place each card deck face-down in a separate pile in the center of a circle. Choose someone to begin. The first player draws a word card and turns it so all other players can see it. That player then draws a voice card and must speak, sing, or whisper the displayed word, using the designated voice. After each turn, the player places the voice card in the discard pile, and the game continues clockwise with the next player. Players continue to speak, sing, or whisper the displayed word until a "new word" card is drawn. The player who turns up a "new word" card displays the new word and then draws again from the voice card pile. The game lasts as long as time allows.

rocking chair	tennis court	paint brush	french fries
swimming pool	back pack	ice cubes	banana
peanut butter	boom box	video game	puppy dog

soft	sad	excited	new word
low	happy	angry	new word
high	loud	sleepy	new word

Old Favorites: New Voices

Pitch content: Vocal exercise

Suggested grade level(s): K to 3

Formation: Teacher's choice

Materials required:

- "New Voices" page (master 1–10)

Preparation:

Use the "New Voices" page as a master to make an overhead transparency or duplicate one copy for each student.

Procedure:

Choose a song that is familiar to the class, such as "Twinkle, Twinkle, Little Star," or "Mary Had a Little Lamb." Explain to the class that you will perform the song in different voices. Experiment with singing, speaking, whispering, and shouting the lyrics to the song. (NOTE: Use shouting as an option sparingly and guardedly. Children merely need to label the shouting voice and differentiate between shouting and singing. Make students aware that shouting can do harm to the vocal mechanism.)

Other ideas:

1. Choose a child to sing, speak, whisper, or shout a favorite song, changing voices every phrase or two. Instruct the class members to signal their identification of each voice used, using the "New Voices" page.
2. Use hand puppets. (See the next activity, "Puppet Voices.") Perform the song in its entirety using one voice, and then switch puppets and repeat the song in another voice.
3. Use hand puppets, but switch puppets and voices more frequently, such as after every two phrases.
4. Allow several students to come forward and wear the puppets. They will hide the puppets behind a table or chair, and show only one at a time. The class will perform the song in the voice designated by the visible puppet.

sing

shout

whisper

speak

Puppet Voices

Pitch content: Vocal exercise

Suggested grade level(s): preK to 2

Formation: Teacher's choice

Materials required:

- hand puppets (purchased or handmade)
- necklace patterns (master 1–11)

Preparation:

Duplicate the necklace patterns. Cut out the circles and punch holes as indicated. Color the circles and laminate them for longer wear. Thread yarn or string through the holes to make necklaces for the hand puppets.

Procedure:

Hang a necklace around the neck of each puppet: WHISPER, SING, TALK, and SHOUT. (NOTE: Use shouting as an option sparingly and guardedly. Children merely need to label the shouting voice and differentiate between shouting and singing. Make students aware that shouting can do harm to the vocal mechanism.)

Use one puppet at a time. Speak, sing, whisper, or shout a phrase or sentence to the class. Students echo in the voice indicated on the puppet's necklace. Be sure to change the puppets frequently.

Other ideas:

1. Use the puppets to ask questions of the class. Student responses must match the voices used by the puppets. Give all instructions in the voice indicated on the puppet's necklace.
2. Choose a student to talk to the class using one of the puppets.
3. Choose several students to put puppets on their hands and have a conversation. Instruct each child to use the voice indicated on his or her puppet.
4. Meet your students at the door of the music room wearing one of the puppets on your hand. Allow students to enter only after asking permission in the designated voice. Use a different puppet for permission to leave the room.
5. Organize a "Show and Tell" or "Sharing" activity. Allow students to bring treasures and stories from home to share with the class. Sharing volunteers choose a puppet to wear, and all sharing will be done in the voice designated on the puppet.

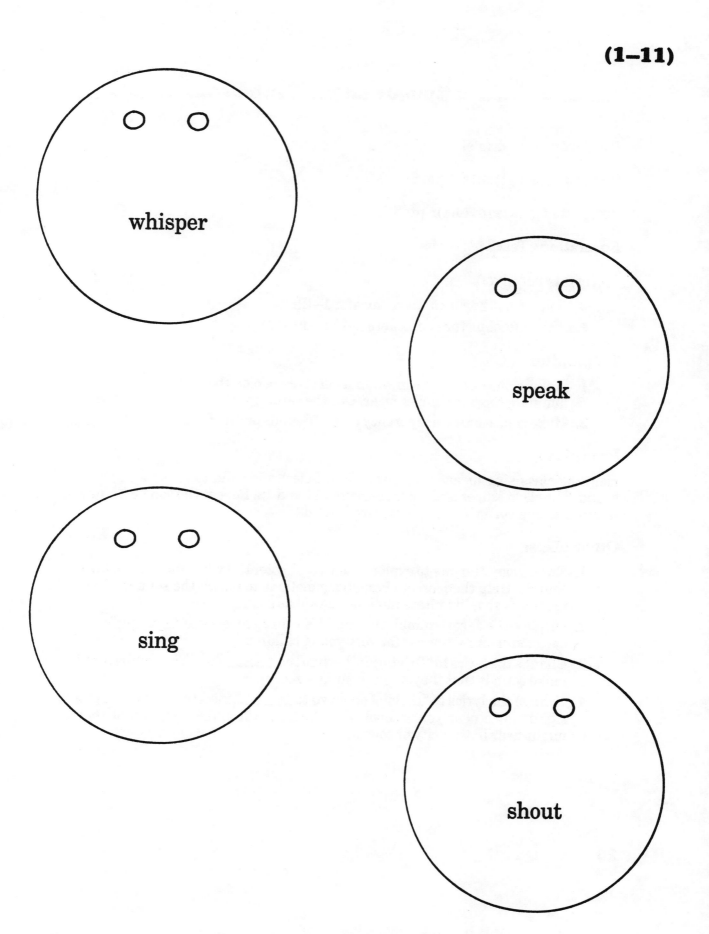

Sounds on the Farm

Pitch content: drmfsl

Predominant pitch(es)/pattern(s): sm

Suggested grade level(s): preK to 2

Formation: Teacher's choice

Materials required:
- "Sounds on the Farm" page (master 1–12)
- farm animal pictures (masters 1–13 and 1–14)

Preparation:
1. Make copies of the farm animal pictures. Color the pictures and then laminate them for longer wear. Cut the cards apart.
2. Make copies or a transparency of the "Sounds on the Farm" page.

Procedure:

Help the class sing measures 1 through 8. Select one child to make an animal sound. The class echoes and sings measures 11 and 12. Repeat the song with new sound-maker soloists as many times as desired.

Other ideas:
1. Encourage students to explore their vocal potential when making up farm sounds. Help them create hand/body motions to match the sounds. Class members should imitate motions as well as sounds.
2. Display the farm animal pictures. Use three at a time to simplify the decision-making process for very young children.
3. Change the lyrics to "Driving on down to the _____ Zoo." The children will make sounds that they might hear at a zoo.
4. Change the lyrics to "Driving on down to _____," inserting the name of a city or town near your school. The children will make sounds that they might hear in that city or town.

Sounds on the Farm

(1–12)

Class:

Driv - ing on down to Grand - pa's farm.___ Driv - ing on down to

Grand - pa's farm.___ Driv - ing on down to Grand - pa's farm.___

Solo: Class: Solo:

What sound will we hear? (Moo ~) (Moo ~) That is what we'll hear.

This Is My Speaking Voice

Pitch content: Vocal exercise

Suggested grade level(s): K to 3

Materials required:

- "This Is My Speaking Voice" page (master 1–15)

Preparation:

Use the "This Is My Speaking Voice" page as a master to make an overhead transparency or duplicate one copy for each student.

Procedure:

Speak, whisper, sing, and shout each line in specified voices. (NOTE: Use shouting as an option sparingly and guardedly. Children merely need to label the shouting voice and differentiate between shouting and singing. Make students aware that shouting can do harm to the vocal mechanism.) The class echoes the words and imitates the voice, pitch, inflection, rhythm, and dynamics used.

Other ideas:

1. Choose a student to be the leader when students know the rhyme well.
2. Ad lib sentences for the students to echo. Use speaking, whispering, and singing voices. Topics might include school, television, books they've read, a favorite sports team, etc. Ask questions requiring a response in a matching voice.

This Is My Speaking Voice (1–15)

L = Leader   C = Class

L: This is my speaking voice.

C: This is my speaking voice.

L: I use it every day.

C: I use it every day.

L: This is my whisper voice.

C: This is my whisper voice.

L: It's quiet, don't you say?

C: It's quiet, don't you say?

L: This is my shouting voice.

C: This is my shouting voice.

L: I use it to shout, "HEY!"

C: I use it to shout, "HEY!"

s m m   s   s   m

L: This is my singing voice.

s m m   s   s   m

C: This is my singing voice.

m s   s   m   m s

L: I like it, it's OK.

m s   s   m   m s

C: I like it, it's OK.

Voice Experiments

Pitch content: Vocal exercise

Suggested grade level(s): 3 and 4

Formation: Small groups

Materials required:
- instruction sheet for each group (master 1–16)
- a pencil for each group

Preparation:

Make a copy of the master for each small group.

Procedure:

Divide the class into groups of three members each. Give each group an instruction sheet and one pencil. Instruct each group to follow the instructions carefully, and to return the sheet when they have finished.

Other ideas:
1. Let each group choose a word or phrase to perform. Instruct the students to experiment with the word, and write down as many ways as they found to sing or speak the word.
2. Follow the instructions on the sheet as a large group. Give each child in the class a chance to try as many voices as possible.

26

Group # _____

Members _____

_____

_____

Instructions:

1. Give each group member a number, 1, 2, or 3.
2. Take turns saying the words "COOKIE JAR." Number one starts first. Each group member should try to say or sing the words differently.
3. Take turns saying "PEPPERONI PIZZA." Each person in the group will try each of the following voices. Place a ✔ in the blank when everyone has tried a voice.

_____ high singing voice
_____ low singing voice
_____ high speaking voice
_____ low speaking voice
_____ angry speaking voice
_____ soft singing voice
_____ loud singing voice
_____ an excited speaking voice
_____ a sleepy speaking voice

4. Return your instruction sheet to your teacher.

I've Heard That Sound Before

Pitch content: Vocal exercise

Suggested grade level(s): preK to 2

Formation: Teacher's choice

Materials needed:

- sounds sheet (master 1–17)

Preparation:

Make a copy of the sounds sheet for each student.

Procedure:

Distribute copies of the sounds sheet to the students. Make one of the sounds depicted on the sheet. Instruct students to point to the picture that matches your sound. Continue with other sounds.

Other ideas:

1. Make only a few sounds yourself. Then choose a student to take over your job as the sound-maker. That student can then choose another student to take his or her place after making three or four sounds.
2. Allow each child a chance to make sounds. After each sound, class members should point to the matching picture.
3. Add a class response after each sound. The sound-maker makes a sound. The class points to the matching picture, and then imitates the sound as a group.

2

Songs and Games to Help Children Learn to Sing in Tune

The great majority of our students can already sing. Their abilities to sing in tune, however, are as varied as their personalities. The objective of this section is improvement in singing accuracy. The songs, games, and activities that follow will meet the diverse needs of your students. They include pitch patterns of variable length, interval content, range, and difficulty. The subject matter, and consequently the age-appeal of each song, is designed to coincide with level of difficulty.

Songs for Beginning and Ending the Music Class

Pitch content: s,l,t,drs

Predominant pitch(es)/pattern(s): s,d

Suggested grade level(s): K to 3

Formation: Teacher's choice

Materials required:
- resonator bells (optional)
- "Hello" page (master 2–1)

Preparation:

Make copies or a transparency of the "Hello" page.

Suggested procedure:

Sing measure 1. The class echoes. Leader and class sing measures 3 and 4 together. Leader sings measure 5, class echoes with measure 6, and leader and class sing measures 7 and 8.

Other ideas:

1. Use this song as a standard greeting to begin each class.
2. Have class members suggest ways to say "hello" in other languages. Revise the song, altering the rhythm and/or melody to sing "jambo," "guten tag," or other foreign phrases. Correlate this activity with a social studies unit if possible.
3. Have class members suggest other English ways to say "hello." Revise the song, altering the rhythm and/or melody to sing "good day," "greetings," "howdy," and others.
4. Sing measures 1 and 5, and have the class sing measures 2 and 6 to themselves.
5. Add resonator bells to the "sol, do mi do" pattern of measures 2 and 6.
6. Show younger children how to point to friends on the words "you and you and you."
7. Choose a student to sing the leader parts.

(2–1)

Hello

Tune In

Pitch content: ms

Predominant pitch(es)/pattern(s): sm

Suggested grade level(s): preK to 3

Formation: Teacher's choice

Materials required:
- "Tune In" page (master 2–2)

Preparation:
Make copies or a transparency of the "Tune In" page.

Procedure:
Begin the class period with this song. Sing measures 1 and 2. The students echo.

Other ideas:
1. Use Curwen hand signs and encourage students to imitate them as they sing.
2. Use this song to improve students' inner hearing skills. Instruct them to (1) listen to you sing, (2) hear the pattern inside their heads, and (3) echo the pattern.
3. Vary the melody from class period to class period. Change the pattern of sol and mi.
4. Vary the melody from class period to class period. Add pitches other than sol and mi:

> sol la sol sol mi
> sol la sol mi do
> sol do' do' do' do'
> mi la sol sol mi

5. Use a sequence of melodies. In addition to the pitch changes, change dynamics from repetition to repetition. A sample sequence follows:

mf	s	m	s	s	m	(students echo)
mf	s	l	s	s	m	(students echo)
mf	s	d′	d′	d′	d′	(students echo)
p	s	m	s	s	m	(students echo)
pp	s	m	s	s	m	(students echo)
whisper	s	m	s	s	m	(students echo)
inner hearing	s	m	s	s	m	(students echo)
mf	s	m	s	s	m	(students echo)

6. Use this song for melodic and rhythmic dictation.

Tune In

Leader: Class:

Tune in, let's be - gin. Tune in, let's be - gin.

Some Love Coffee

Pitch content: drmsl

Predominant pitch(es)/pattern(s): md

Suggested grade level(s): K to 2

Formation: Teacher's choice

Materials required:
- "Some Love Coffee" page (master 2–3)
- disk pattern, optional (master 2–4)

Preparation:
1. If disks are used, make copies of the disk pattern and cut out the disks. Color them and then laminate for longer wear. Glue the disks onto heavy paper or plastic coffee can lids.
2. Make copies or a transparency of the "Some Love Coffee" page.

Suggested procedure:

Sing the song alone as you begin the music class. The class echoes the last phrase "I love the children who sing with me."

Other ideas:
1. Help the class sing measures 1 through 4 with you. Select one student to echo the class and sing measures 5 and 6.
2. Add a second verse to extend the activity:

   > Some love bells when they ring and chime,
   > But I love to know that it's music time.
   > I love to know that it's music time.

3. Instruct students to pass the disk from person to person as they sing. The student holding the disk at the end of measure 4 is the designated soloist.
4. Sing measures 1 and 2. The class echoes. Sing measures 3 and 4. The class echoes.
5. Use the call-and-response format of idea #4. Divide the class in half. Group A sings measures 1 and 2, and group B echoes. Group A sings measures 3 and 4, and group B echoes.

38

Some Love Coffee

Some love cof - fee, Some love tea, but I love the chil - dren who sing with me. I love the chil - dren who sing with me.

2. Some love bells
   When they ring and chime,
   But I love to know
   That it's music time.
   I love to know
   That it's music time.

It's your turn!

Shake My Hand and Say Hello

Pitch content: drmfsl

Predominant pitch(es)/pattern(s): rsd

Suggested grade level(s): preK to 2

Formation: Teacher's choice

Materials required:

- "Shake My Hand and Say Hello" page (master 2–5)

Preparation:

Make copies or a transparency of the "Shake My Hand and Say Hello" page.

Suggested procedure:

Help the class sing measures 1 through 8 as you circulate among the students and shake hands. The child whose hand you are shaking as the class sings measures 7 and 8, "Tell us all your name," is the designated soloist. He or she sings measures 9 and 10. The class responds with measures 11 and 12, and the song is repeated.

Other ideas:

1. Have all of the class members wave to the soloist as they sing the last phrase, "Nice to know your name."
2. Use a hand puppet to circulate and shake hands with students. Very often, the puppet will help inhibited students concentrate more on shaking hands than on nervousness.
3. Allow a student to take your job as the "official handshaker." He or she will circulate around the class and designate a new soloist. The official handshaker will change with every repetition of the song.
4. Use this song to welcome a new student to your class.

(2–5)

Shake My Hand and Say Hello

Class:

Shake my hand and say hel - lo, say hel - lo, say hel - lo.

Shake my hand and say hel - lo. Tell us all your name.

Solo: Class:

(Ka - ri) is my name. Nice to know your name.

If You're Ready

Pitch content: rmfsltd'

Predominant pitch(es)/pattern(s): sltd'

Suggested grade level(s): 1 and 2

Formation: Teacher's choice

Materials required:
- "If You're Ready" page (master 2–6)
- disk pattern, optional (master 2–4), from page 40.

Preparation:
1. If disks are used, make copies of the disk pattern and cut out the disks. Color them and then laminate for longer wear. Glue the disks onto heavy paper or plastic coffee can lids.
2. Make copies or a transparency of the "If You're Ready" page.

Procedure:

Sing the song alone as you begin the music class. Help the class echo the last phrase "Sit up straight and tall."

Other ideas:
1. Help students sing measures 1 through 8 with you. Select one student to echo the class (singing measures 9 and 10).
2. Instruct students to pass the disk from person to person as they sing. The student holding the disk at the end of measure 8 is the designated soloist.
3. Add verses to create a warm-up activity:

    Versus:
    2. If you're ready for music stand and sing,
       Stand and sing, stand and sing.
       If you're ready for music stand and sing,
       Stand and sing WITH ME.
    3. Walk the beat
    4. Tap your head
    5. Rub your tummy
    6. Snap the beat
    7. Clap the beat

43

(2—6)

If You're Ready

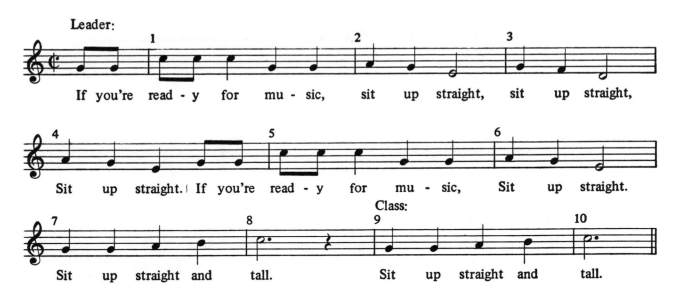

If you're ready for music:
2. Stand and sing with me.
3. Walk the beat with me.
4. Tap your head with me.
5. Rub your tummy with me.
6. Snap the beat with me.
7. Clap the beat with me.

Roll Call

Pitch content: ms

Predominant pitch(es)/pattern(s): sm

Suggested grade level(s): preK to 3

Formation: Circle

Materials required:

- Class list, optional
- "Roll Call" page (master 2–7)

Preparation:

Make copies or a transparency of the "Roll Call" page.

Procedure:

Use these examples as models. Insert your own students' names and adapt melodic and rhythmic notation to create a musical roll call. Call every child's name, and give each one a chance to respond.

Other ideas:

1. Keep the class actively involved. Add a class response after each child's solo. Sing "Her name's _____," or "His name's _____."
2. Change the melody of your calls. Use sol and mi in another pattern.
3. Change the melody of your calls. Add la, do, re, and other pitches to challenge your students' matching skills.
4. Use a variety of patterns in one class period, changing them (a) according to the pitch-matching progress level of each student, or (b) at random.

Roll Call

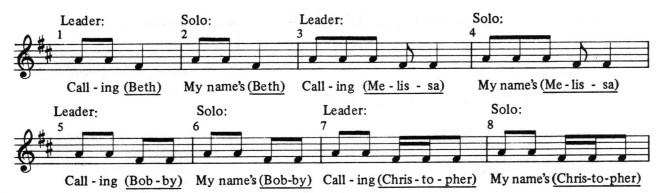

Leader: Solo: Leader: Solo:

Call - ing (Beth)   My name's (Beth)   Call - ing (Me - lis - sa)   My name's (Me - lis - sa)

Leader: Solo: Leader: Solo:

Call - ing (Bob - by)   My name's (Bob-by)   Call - ing (Chris - to - pher)   My name's (Chris-to-pher)

Very Nice to Know You

Pitch content: drmsl

Predominant pitch(es)/pattern(s): sm   smd

Suggested grade level(s): preK to 3

Formation: Teacher's choice

Materials required:
- class list, optional
- "Very Nice to Know You" page (master 2–8)

Preparation:

Make copies or a transparency of the "Very Nice to Know You" page.

Procedure:

Sing measure 1, using the first name of any child in the class. That child responds singing "here!" trying to match the pitches sung by the teacher. The class sings measures 3 and 4. It will be necessary to alter the rhythm of measures 1 and 3 to accommodate some names.

Other ideas:
1. Add movement. Have class members stand whenever they sing their part, and sit as soon as they finish. The quick pop-up action creates a fun movement game.
2. Help each child make up a name and print it on a name card. The made-up names might be famous persons, fictional characters, composers, Halloween characters, or nonsense names.
3. Use last names instead of first names.
4. Have your students trade names.
5. Use this song for taking roll.

Very Nice to Know You

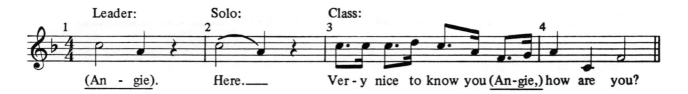

Cheerio

Pitch content: ms

Predominant pitch(es)/pattern(s): sm

Suggested grade level(s): preK to 3

Formation: Teacher's choice

Materials required:

- "Cheerio" page (master 2–9)

Preparation:

Make copies or a transparency of the "Cheerio" student page.

Procedure:

Use as a closing song to end the music class. Sing measures 1 and 2. The students echo.

Other ideas:

1. Use Curwen hand signs and encourage students to imitate them as they sing.
2. Use this song to improve students' inner hearing skills. Instruct them to (a) listen to you sing, (b) hear the pattern inside their heads, and (c) echo the pattern.
3. Vary the melody from class period to class period. Change the pattern of sol and mi.
4. Vary the melody from class period to class period. Add pitches other than sol and mi:

> sol sol la sol sol mi
> sol sol la sol mi do
> sol sol do' do' do' do'
> mi mi la sol sol mi

5. Use a sequence of melodies. In addition to the pitch changes, change dynamics from repetition to repetition. A sample sequence follows:

mf	s	s	m	s	s	m	(students echo)
mf	s	s	l	s	s	m	(students echo)
mf	s	s	d'	d'	d'	d'	(students echo)
p	s	s	m	s	s	m	(students echo)
pp	s	s	m	s	s	m	(students echo)
whisper	s	s	m	s	s	m	(students echo)
inner hearing	s	s	m	s	s	m	(students echo)
mf	s	s	m	s	s	m	(students echo)

6. Use this song for melodic and rhythmic dictation.

Cheerio

Leader: Cheer - i - o, Time to go. Class: Cheer - i - o, Time to go.

Auf Wiedersehen

Pitch content: drmfs

Predominant pitch(es)/pattern(s): sm

Suggested grade level(s): K to 4

Formation: Teacher's choice

Materials required:
- resonator bells, optional
- "Auf Wiedersehen" page (master 2–10)

Preparation:

Make copies or a transparency of the "Auf Wiedersehen" page.

Procedure:

Leader sings measure 1. The class echoes. Leader and class sing measures 3 and 4 together. Leader sings measure 5. The class echoes with measure 6. Leader and class sing measures 7 and 8.

Other ideas:
1. Use this song as a standard closing for the class period.
2. Select one student to sing the echo parts (measures 2 and 6) as a solo.
3. Have class members suggest ways to say "good-bye" in other languages. Revise the song, altering the rhythm and/or melody to sing "au revoir," "ciao," "arrivederci," and other foreign phrases. Correlate this activity with a social studies unit if possible.
4. Have class members suggest other English ways to say "good-bye." Revise the song, altering the rhythm and/or melody to sing "cheerio," "farewell," "be seeing you," and other phrases.
5. Sing measures 1 and 5. Have the class sing measures 2 and 6 to themselves.
6. Add resonator bells to the "sol-mi" pattern of measures 2 and 6.
7. Choose a student to sing the leader parts.

52

Auf Wiedersehen

Leader: Class: All:

Auf   wie - der-seh'n, Auf   wie - der-seh'n, Auf   wie - der - seh'n we   say.

Leader: Class: All:

Auf   wie - der-seh'n, Auf   wie - der-seh'n, We'll   see you   an - oth - er   day.

Holiday/Seasonal Songs

Halloween

Pitch content: l,t,drr#m

Predominant pitch(es)/pattern(s): mrdt,l,

Suggested grade level(s): K to 3

Formation: Teacher's choice

Materials required:

- "Halloween" page (master 2–11)

Preparation:

Make copies or a transparency of the "Halloween" page.

Suggested procedure:

Choose a soloist, and announce his or her name to the class. The class sings the song, and inserts the name of the soloist into the question, "What will _____ be?" The soloist responds and inserts the name of his or her Halloween costume. The class ends the song with "He (She) will be a _____," echoing the soloist.

Other ideas:

1. Change the "He (She)" in the final response to the soloist's name, such as "Kari will be a ghost."
2. Give each soloist a halloween treat or sticker.
3. Change the soloist's response to "Guess what I will be." The soloist then points to members of the class, who try to guess his or her costume. When someone guesses correctly, the class sings the final response, "He (She) will be a _____."
4. Try improvised musical conversation between the soloist and the members of the class while using the guessing game described in Idea 3.

(2–11)

Halloween

Class:
Hal - lo - ween, Hal - lo - ween, Strang - est night I've ev - er seen.

Hal - lo - ween, Hal - lo - ween. What will (Jen - ny) be?

Solo: Class:

What will (Jen - ny) be? I will be a (princess). S/He will be a (princess).

Tutti Frutti Monsters

Pitch content: msl

Predominant pitch(es)/pattern(s): smlsm

Suggested grade level(s): 2 to 4

Formation: Teacher's choice

Materials required:

- "Tutti Frutti Monsters" page (master 2–12)
- disk pattern, optional (master 2–4) from page 40.

Preparation:

1. If disks are used, make copies of the disk pattern and cut out the disks. Color them and then laminate for longer wear. Glue the disks onto heavy paper or plastic coffee can lids.
2. Make copies or a transparency of the "Tutti Frutti Monsters" page.

Suggested procedure:

Use this as a variation to "Tutti Frutti Ice Cream" (see "Songs for General Use" section). Instruct each child to imagine him- or herself as a monster, and decide what monster he or she would be. Help the class sing measures 1 through 8. While they are singing, select one child to stand and sing the solo. Repeat the song with a new soloist.

Other ideas:

1. Make the song cumulative by "saving solos." For example, soloist #1 sings "Frankenstein looks like me." The song is repeated. Soloist #2 sings "Dracula looks like me," and soloist #1 sings again "Frankenstein looks like me." After the third repetition of the song, three soloists sing, etc.
2. Allow every child a chance to sing a solo by taking turns around the classroom. Use this method with or without the cumulative ending.
3. Seat students in a circle. While singing, they pass the disk from person to person. The student who is holding the disk at measure 9 sings his or her solo. Use this option with or without the cumulative ending.
4. Use Idea 3 in classroom formation.

57

5. Use sound effects (either recorded or student-created) for an introduction and a coda.

6. Help the class create a spoken ostinato to use with the song. "Tutti frutti monsters" or "Dancing 'round the tree" would be good possibilities.

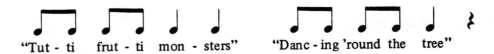

"Tut - ti   frut - ti   mon - sters"   "Danc - ing 'round the   tree"

Tutti Frutti Monsters

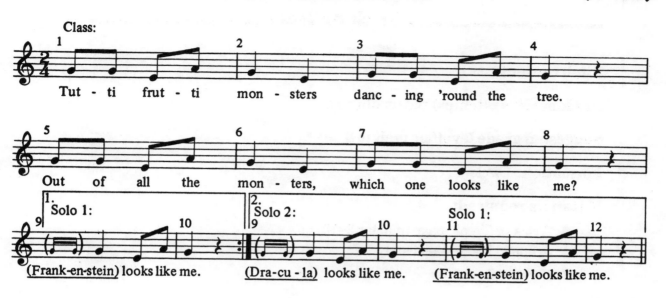

Class:

1 · 2 · 3 · 4
Tut - ti frut - ti mon - sters danc - ing 'round the tree.

5 · 6 · 7 · 8
Out of all the mon - sters, which one looks like me?

1. Solo 1:
9 · 10
(Frank-en-stein) looks like me.

2. Solo 2:
9 · 10
(Dra-cu - la) looks like me.

Solo 1:
11 · 12
(Frank-en-stein) looks like me.

Trick or Treat

Pitch content: ms

Predominant pitch(es)/pattern(s): sm

Suggested grade level(s): preK to 3

Formation: Circle

Materials required:
- "Trick or Treat" page (master 2–13)
- wrapped Halloween candy
- paper bag

Preparation:

Make copies or a transparency of the "Trick or Treat" student page.

Suggested procedure:

Distribute candy to the class members. Choose one child to carry the trick-or-treat sack and move around the inside of the circle as the class sings. To choose a soloist, the trick-or-treater stops in front of one child at measure 4. The soloist sings measures 5 and 6 and drops his or her candy into the sack. The trick-or-treater sings the "thank you" solo and takes a place in the circle. The soloist becomes the new trick-or-treater, and the song is repeated. When the song is ended, make sure that each child gets one piece of candy to eat.

Other ideas:

1. Adapt a response for a child who has given his or her candy away. The child might sing "I'm all out of candy." The trick-or-treater might sing "Have a Happy Halloween," and keep the trick-or-treat sack until he or she finds someone who has some candy.
2. Dramatize trick-or-treating. Choose three or four children to go off to corners of the room into imaginary houses. Choose a trick-or-treater to walk up to each "house," knock at the "door," and sing the song.
3. Use a game similar to "London Bridge." One child has a bag full of candy. Two children form a bridge. Students move around in a circle, under the bridge. When the class sings measure 4, the bridge falls and traps one child. The child with the candy bag sings the solo (measures 5 and 6), and gives the trapped child a piece of candy. The trapped child sings the "thank you" solo, takes the place of the candy-giver, and the song begins again.

Trick or Treat

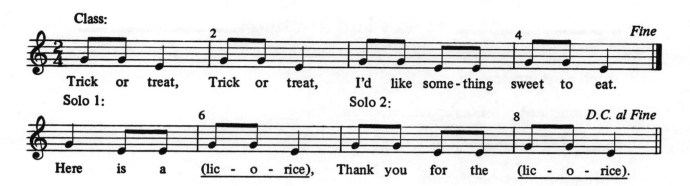

Class:

Trick or treat, Trick or treat, I'd like some-thing sweet to eat.

Solo 1:   Solo 2:

Here is a (lic - o - rice), Thank you for the (lic - o - rice).

Turkey and Stuffing

Pitch content: ms

Predominant pitch(es)/pattern(s): sm

Suggested grade level(s): K to 3

Formation: Teacher's choice

Materials required:
- "Turkey and Stuffing" page (master 2–14)
- disk pattern, optional (master 2–14) from page 40.

Preparation:
1. If disks are used, make copies of the disk pattern and cut out the disks. Color them and then laminate for longer wear. Glue the disks onto heavy paper or plastic coffee can lids.
2. Make copies or a transparency of the "Turkey and Stuffing" page.

Suggested procedure:

Help children prepare solos about their favorite foods at a turkey dinner. Help the class sing the song. Select one student to sing solo 1. Repeat the song as many times as desired.

Other ideas:
1. Pass the disk from person to person as you sing. The child holding the disk when the song ends is the designated soloist.
2. Make the song cumulative by "saving solos." For example, soloist #1 sings "I like the rolls." The song is repeated. Soloist #2 sings "I like the turkey," and soloist #1 sings again "I like the rolls." After the third repetition of the song, three soloists sing, etc.
3. Allow each child a chance to sing a solo. Take turns going around the classroom. Use this method with or without the cumulative ending.

Turkey and Stuffing

Spin the Dreidel

Pitch content: l,t,drm

Predominant pitch(es)/pattern(s): mrdt,l,

Suggested grade level(s): preK to 3

Formation: Teacher's choice

Materials required:
- "Spin the Dreidel" page (master 2–15)
- paper dreidel, optional (master 2–16)
- real dreidel, optional

Preparation:
1. If the paper dreidel is used, make a copy of the pattern and cut it out. Color the dreidel and laminate for longer use. Glue onto heavy paper or plastic coffee can lid.
2. Make copies or a transparency of the "Spin the Dreidel" page.

Suggested procedure:

Help the class sing measures 1 through 4. Select one student to sing measure 5 as a solo. Repeat the song with a new soloist.

Other ideas:
1. Use the paper dreidel. Students will pass it from person to person as they sing. The child holding the dreidel at the end of measure 4 will sing the solo.
2. Pass a real dreidel from child to child as the song is sung.
3. Allow each soloist to spin the real dreidel after singing his or her solo.
4. Correlate with the study of the Hanukkah story and Hanukkah songs.

Spin the Dreidel

(2–15)

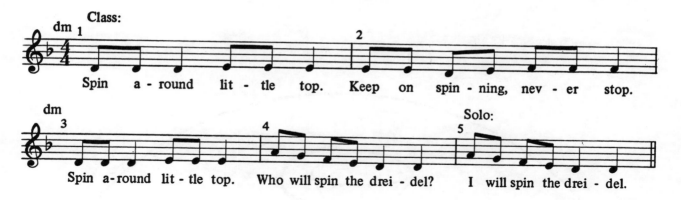

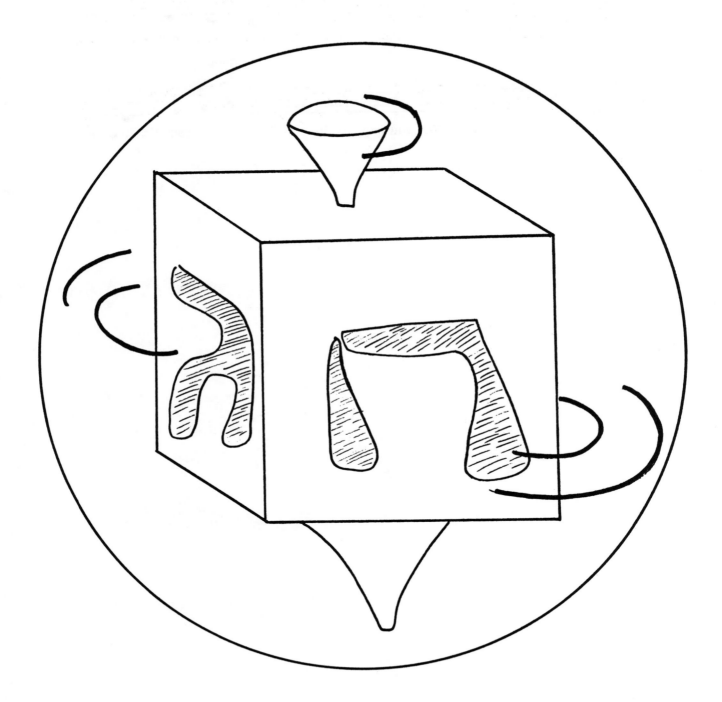

Santa Needs Another Elf

Pitch content: drmfsl

Predominant pitch(es)/pattern(s): smlsm   sfmrd

Suggested grade level(s): preK to 2

Formation: Circle

Materials required:
- "Santa Needs Another Elf" page (master 2–17)
- elf badges, optional (master 2–18)
- resonator bells, optional
- beanbag, optional

Preparation:
1. If the elf badges are used, make enough patterns for each student to receive a badge. Color the badges and cut them out. Laminate for longer use.
2. Make copies or a transparency of the "Santa Needs Another Elf" page.

Suggested procedure:

Play this game as you would "London Bridge." Choose two class members to hold hands in an arch and make a bridge. Help the class members form a circle and sing the song, stepping the beat as they pass under the bridge. As the class sings "Who will volunteer?" the bridge falls. The child caught inside sings the solo. He or she becomes part of the bridge and the song is repeated.

Other ideas:
1. Play this game in regular classroom formation. Select a child to sing the solo. That soloist chooses the next soloist, etc.
2. Choose a leader to stand in the center of a circle holding a beanbag. The leader tosses the beanbag to a person he or she chooses to be the soloist. The soloist becomes the new "tosser" as the song begins again.
3. Add resonator bells to the question-and-answer parts.
4. Give an elf badge to everyone who volunteers to help Santa.

(2—17)   **Santa Needs Another Elf**

San - ta needs an - oth - er elf,   San - ta needs an - oth - er elf.

San - ta needs an-oth - er elf,   Who will vol - un-teer?   I will vol - un-teer.

SANTA'S HELPER

SANTA'S HELPER

SANTA'S HELPER

Christmas Train

Pitch content: dmfsltd′

Predominant pitch(es)/pattern(s): smlsm

Suggested grade level(s): preK to 2

Formation: Circle

Materials required:

- "Christmas Train" page (master 2–19)

Preparation:

Make copies or a transparency of the "Christmas Train" page.

Suggested procedure:

Choose one child to lead a human train and walk around the outside of the circle. As the class sings "What do you want for Christmas?" the leader chooses a soloist by stopping behind a classmate. The soloist sings measures 7 and 8, naming an item from his or her Christmas "wish list." After the solo, the song begins again and the soloist joins the train.

Other ideas:

1. Change the spirit of the song by changing the question. Revise the words to "What are you giving for Christmas?" Possible answers might be "I'm giving my brother a truck"; "I'm giving my mom a hug"; "I'm giving my sister a doll."
2. Play the game in a regular classroom setting, with children seated at desks or in chairs. The train travels up and down the aisles, stopping beside soloists' desks.

Christmas Train

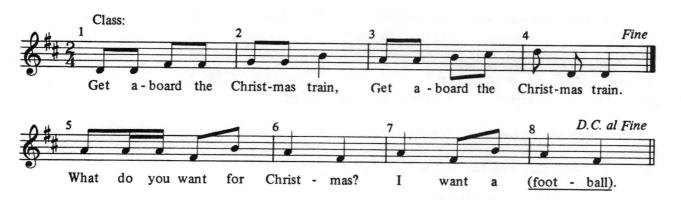

Get a-board the Christ-mas train, Get a-board the Christ-mas train.

What do you want for Christ - mas? I want a (foot - ball).

Special Valentine

Pitch content: drmfs

Predominant pitch(es)/pattern(s): sd smrd

Suggested grade level(s): 1 to 3

Formation: Teacher's choice

Materials required:

- "Special Valentine" page (master 2–20)
- paper hearts, optional (master 2–21)
- box, basket, or paper bag, optional
- beanbag, optional

Preparation:

1. If the paper hearts are used, make enough for each student to receive one. Color the hearts and cut them out. Laminate for longer use.
2. Make copies or a transparency of the "Special Valentine" page.

Suggested procedure:

Distribute paper hearts to each child. Instruct students to write their names on the hearts and deposit them in a Valentine Mailbox (box, basket, or paper bag). Draw one name as the class sings the song. The child whose name is selected sings the solo, and gets to draw the next name out of the mailbox.

Other ideas:

1. Play the game without paper hearts. Select a child to sing the solo. That soloist chooses the next soloist, etc.
2. Stand in the center of a circle and toss a beanbag to designate a soloist. The soloist becomes the new "tosser" as the song begins again.
3. Help the students make up names and print them on name cards. The made-up names might be famous persons, fictional characters, composers, cartoon characters, or nonsense names. Only the person who wrote each name will know when his or her card is drawn. Each soloist names a character to whom his or her made-up character would send a special Valentine.
4. Use last names instead of first names.
5. Have students trade names.

72

Special Valentine

Class:
If (Ka-tie) had a spe-cial Val-en - tine, If (Ka-tie) had a spe-cial

Val - en - tine, If (Ka-tie) had a spe-cial Val-en - tine, I

Solo:
won - der who'd s/he'd send it to? I'd send it to my (moth - er).

(2–21)

Pitch content: drmfsl

Predominant pitch(es)/pattern(s): sm   rs   md

Suggested grade level(s): K to 3

Formation: Teacher's choice

Materials required:
- "Peter Rabbit" page (master 2–22)
- eight vegetable cards (masters 2–23 and 2–24)

Preparation:
1. Make copies of the vegetable cards. Color the cards and cut them apart. Laminate for longer use.
2. Make copies or a transparency of the "Peter Rabbit" page.

Suggested procedure:

Distribute vegetable cards to eight different students. The class sings the song, allowing the eight cardholders to respond to their own vegetable solos. When the song is over, the eight soloists give their cards to other students and the song begins again.

Other ideas:
1. Simplify the song by using only four vegetable cards.
2. Choose one soloist who sings all eight solos.
3. Have each soloist stand when he or she sings a solo.
4. Divide the class into two groups. Designate one group to sing the class part, and the other to sing the solo part. This will create a two-part echo effect.
5. Try other ways of dividing the class: boys/girls, blue eyes/brown eyes, those who like spinach/those who do not like spinach, etc. Use these groups to echo each other as they sing names of the vegetables.
6. Correlate with the story *Peter Rabbit*.

Peter Rabbit

Class:

1 · 2 · 3

Pe - ter Rab - bit aw - ful bad. Found the gar - den

4 · 5 · 6 · 7

gate. What a tum - my - ache he had. here is what he

Solo: · Class: · Solo: · Class: · Solo:

8 · 9 · 10

ate, *munch, munch, munch,* Car - rots, car - rots, Mush - rooms, mush - rooms,

Class: · Solo: · Class: · Solo: · Class: · Solo:

11 · 12 · 13

Cab - bage, cab - bage, Cel - er - y, cel - er - y, Tur - nips, tur - nips,

Class: · Solo: · Class: · Solo: · Class: · Solo:

14 · 15 · 16

On - ions, on - ions, Let - tuce, let - tuce, Broc - co - li, broc - co - li.

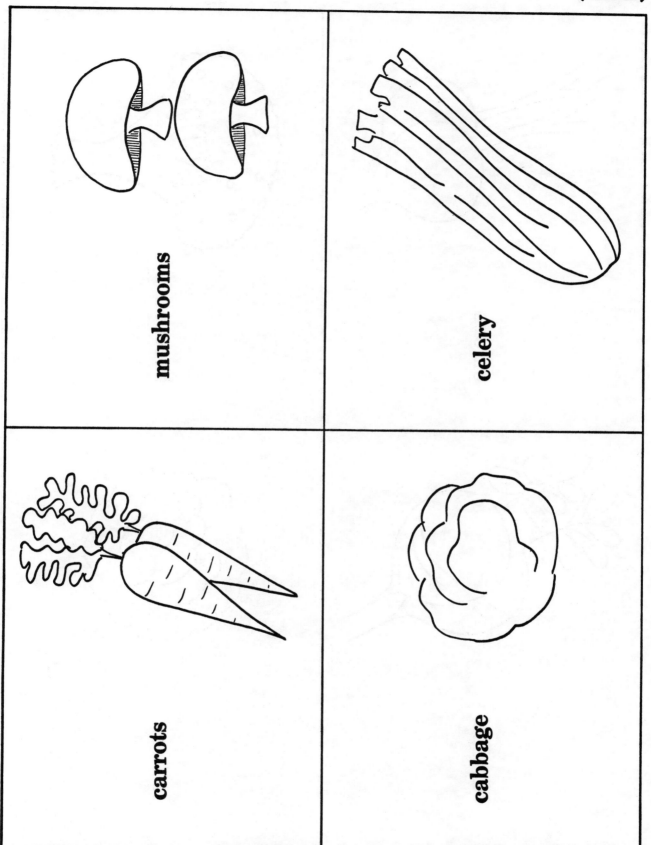

mushrooms

celery

carrots

cabbage

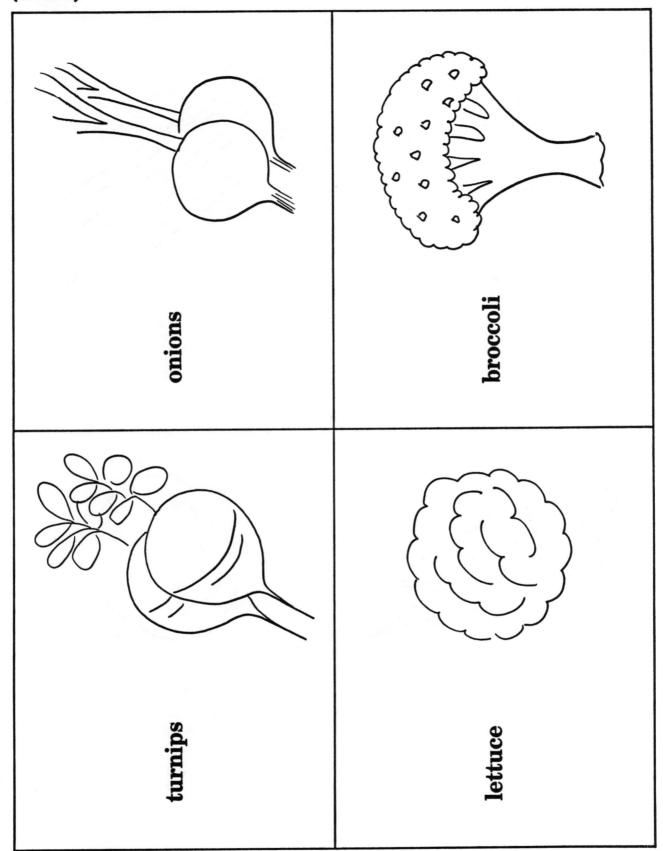

onions

broccoli

turnips

lettuce

Songs for the Older Elementary Student

Pitch content: dmsld'

Predominant pitch(es)/pattern(s): mlsl

Suggested grade level(s): 3 to 5

Formation: Circle or classroom formation

Materials required:
- "A-B-C Safari" page (master 2–25)

Preparation:

Make copies or a transparency of the "A-B-C Safari" page.

Suggested procedure:

Assign one letter of the alphabet to each member of the class in alphabetical order around the circle or room. (It's a good idea to take the letter A for yourself.) Give students time to think of words for their letters and prepare their solos. Begin the song with the A soloist (measure 1). The class echoes the solo (measure 2). The class sings measures 3 and 4 together. Continue the song with the B soloist, class echoing with measure 6. The class sings measures 7 and 8. The song continues with the C soloist, etc.

Other ideas:

1. Specify a category to which all A-B-C words must belong. The printed example (using animals) is one possibility.
2. Assign letters in random order around the classroom or circle.
3. Try a variation using partners instead of the whole class. Partner one begins by singing measure 1, inserting any noun that begins with letter A; partner two echoes (measure 2); both sing measures 3 and 4; partner one sings measure 5; partner two echoes (measure 6); both sing measures 7 and 8. The object is to have partner one go as far as he or she can in the entire alphabet without missing a letter or a beat. When he or she makes a mistake, partner two takes over as the leader and begins with letter A. Each tries to go further than his or her partner did. Both partners work together to get through the entire alphabet.
4. Add a hand clapping pattern; for example, tap knees (one time), clap hands (one time), clap partner's hands (two times).
5. Make the clapping pattern more difficult. Add right and left hand patterns, with partners slapping each other's right hands, followed by slapping each other's left hands.

A-B-C Safari

A (an aard-vark), A (an aard-vark), That's what A is for.

B (a but-ter-fly), B (a but-ter-fly), Now let's do some more.

2. C, A CAMEL
   D, A DINOSAUR

3. E, AN ELEPHANT
   F, A FIREFLY

4. G, A GOLDFISH
   H, A HONEYBEE

5. I, AN INSECT
   J, A JAGUAR

6. K, A KANGAROO
   L, A LION

7. M, A MONKEY
   N, A NIGHTINGALE

8. O, AN OSTRICH
   P, A PARAKEET

9. Q, A QUAIL
   R, A RABBIT

10. S, A SPIDER
    T, A TURTLE

11. U, A UNICORN
    V, A VULTURE

12. W, A WALRUS
    X, A XIPHIAS

13. Y, A YAK
    Z, A ZEBRA

Baseball, Baseball

Pitch content: fsltd'

Predominant pitch(es)/pattern(s): sltd'   d'   sls

Suggested grade level(s): 4 and 5

Formation: Circle

Materials required:
- "Baseball, Baseball" page (master 2–26)
- ball patterns (master 2–27)
- real baseball, optional
- blank cards, optional
- hat, can, bag, or box, optional

Preparation:
1. If the ball pattern is used, make a copy of the master and cut out the ball. Color and then laminate for longer wear. Glue the pattern onto heavy paper.
2. Make copies or a transparency of the "Baseball, Baseball" page.

Suggested procedure:

Instruct each student to choose a major league baseball team to sing about. It is helpful to list teams on the board, and allow students to choose from the list. As the students sing the song, they pass a baseball (real or a pattern) from one person to the next. The student holding the ball at the end of measure 8 will sing the solo. That student inserts the name of his or her favorite team. The soloist passes the baseball to the next person and the song is repeated.

Other ideas:
1. Adapt the game for football, basketball, or another sport. (See master 2–27 for two other ball patterns.)
2. Add a class response after each solo, using the solo melody (sol sol la ti do' do' do'). The lyrics might be "Dodgers is the team she picks."
3. Ask students to suggest names of teams, and write them on blank cards. Place all cards in a hat, can, bag, or box. Pass the hat around the circle as the class sings. The person holding the hat at measure 8 will draw a team and sing about it.

Baseball, Baseball

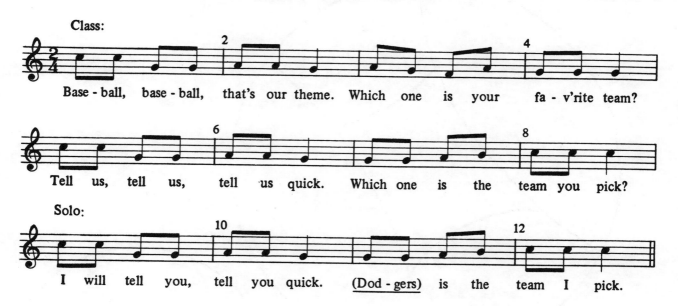

Class:

Base - ball, base - ball, that's our theme. Which one is your fa - v'rite team?

Tell us, tell us, tell us quick. Which one is the team you pick?

Solo:

I will tell you, tell you quick. (Dod - gers) is the team I pick.

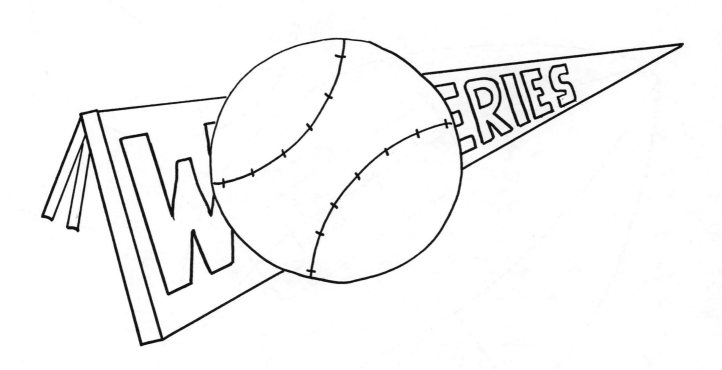

(2–27)

Calling Your Number

Pitch content: msl

Predominant pitch(es)/pattern(s): ml

Suggested grade level(s): 3 to 5

Formation: Circle

Materials required:

- "Calling Your Number" page (master 2–28)

Preparation:

Make copies or a transparency of the "Calling Your Number" page.

Suggested procedure:

Give each student a number, beginning with number one, in sequence around the circle. Students sing measures 1 through 3. Number one is the first soloist. He or she sings measure 4 and calls a number to choose the next soloist. Repeat the song. The game continues as long as every student listens for his or her number and is ready to call out another person's number.

Other ideas:

1. Specify that a student will be out if he or she is not ready with a number. He or she will sit in the center of the circle BUT ONLY until another student is out. Number one restarts the game.
2. Make concentration more difficult by renumbering after a person is made out. The object of the game is to become Number One.
3. Try a name version. See "Calling Angie" on master 2–28. The soloist sings measure 1. The class joins the soloist for measures 2 through 4.

(2–28)   # Calling Your Number

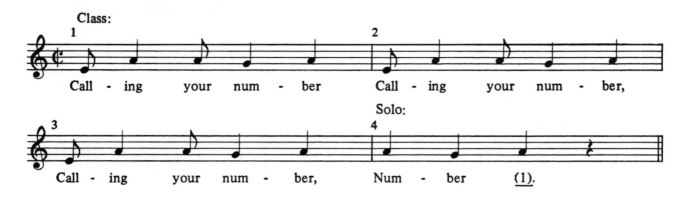

Calling Angie

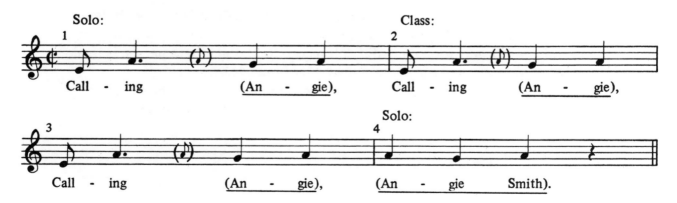

One Potato, Two

Pitch content: drmsl

Predominant pitch(es)/pattern(s): dlsl

Suggested grade level(s): 2 to 4

Formation: Teacher's choice

Materials required:

- "One Potato, Two" page (master 2–29)

Preparation:

Make copies or a transparency of the "One Potato, Two" page.

Suggested procedure:

Help the class sing the song inserting the name of any student in the blank (measure 3). As the class continues singing, the selected student prepares a name to insert in the blank (measure 7). As the song is repeated, each named person supplies the name of a new classmate for the upcoming blank.

Other ideas:

1. Extend the length of each solo. Each soloist will sing (on do la sol) "_____ just walked." The class will join the soloist in singing the remainder of the phrase, "through the music room door."
2. Extend the solo further. Each soloist will sing "_____ just walked through the music room door," or "_____ just walked through the garden gate."
3. Divide the class into two groups for call-and-response singing. The first group sings measures 1 and 2, and 5 and 6. The second group responds with measures 3 and 4, and 7 and 8. Exchange parts and repeat the song.

One Potato, Two

Class:

One po - ta - to, Two po - ta - to, Three po - ta - to, four.

Solo: Class:

(Jen - ny) just walked through the mu - sic room door.

Five po - ta - to, Six po - ta - to, Sev'n po - ta - to, eight.

Solo: Class:

(Rob - bie) just walked through the gar - den gate.

Rico's Pizza Restaurant

Pitch content: drmsl

Predominant pitch(es)/pattern(s): ms

Suggested grade level(s): 3 to 5

Formation: Teacher's choice

Materials required:
- "Rico's Pizza Restaurant" page (master 2–30)
- order blanks (master 2–31)
- pencil
- telephone, optional
- telephone bell, optional

Preparation:
1. Make copies of the order blanks and cut them apart.
2. Make copies or a transparency of the "Rico's Pizza Restaurant" page.

Suggested procedure:

Instruct each child to prepare to order a pizza, deciding on size, topping, and kind of crust. Select an order taker, who will stand at a desk and write the order when it is given over the phone. Select a customer, who will stand at the "phone booth" (with toy or imaginary phone) and call with a pizza order. The class sings measures 1 through 8, and asks questions in measures 9 through 14. The customer answers each question. The order-taker fills out an order blank. When the order is completed, the class sings "Thank you for your order." The order-taker and the customer both choose other students to take their places, and the song begins again.

Other ideas:
1. Extend solo opportunities in the song. Have the order-taker sing the questions in measures 9 through 14.
2. Add a telephone sound effect at the beginning of the song.
3. Use this song to introduce an exercise in commercial writing and composing.

(2–30)   **Rico's Pizza Restaurant**

Class:
1. 2. 3. 4.
Ri - co's Piz - za Res - tau - rant, An - y piz - za that you want.

5. 6. 7. 8. *Fine*
All our pies have ex - tra cheese. May I take your or - der please?

Class: Solo: Class: Solo:
9. 10. 11. 12.
What size? (Large) What top - ping? (Pepperoni)

Class: Solo: Class: *D.C. al Fine*
13. 14. 15. 16.
What crust? (Thick crust) Thank you for your or - der.

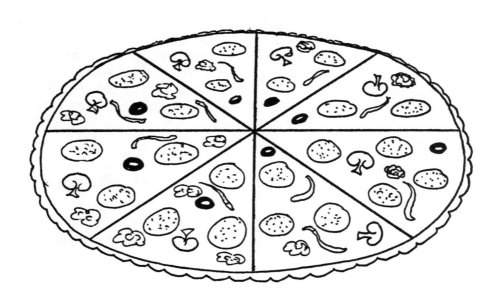

RICO'S PIZZA RESTAURANT

WHAT SIZE?   S   M   L

WHAT TOPPING?   pepperoni   beef

sausage   mushroom

_____

WHAT CRUST?   thin   thick

_____

THANK YOU FOR YOUR ORDER.

RICO'S PIZZA RESTAURANT

WHAT SIZE?   S   M   L

WHAT TOPPING?   pepperoni   beef

sausage   mushroom

_____

WHAT CRUST?   thin   thick

_____

THANK YOU FOR YOUR ORDER.

RICO'S PIZZA RESTAURANT

WHAT SIZE?   S   M   L

WHAT TOPPING?   pepperoni   beef

sausage   mushroom

_____

WHAT CRUST?   thin   thick

_____

THANK YOU FOR YOUR ORDER.

RICO'S PIZZA RESTAURANT

WHAT SIZE?   S   M   L

WHAT TOPPING?   pepperoni   beef

sausage   mushroom

_____

WHAT CRUST?   thin   thick

_____

THANK YOU FOR YOUR ORDER.

What Would You Like to Play?

Pitch content: rmff#sltd′

Predominant pitch(es)/pattern(s): sltd′

Suggested grade level(s): 3 to 5

Formation: Teacher's choice

Materials required:
- "What Would You Like to Play?" page (master (2–32)
- standard classroom instrument posters, optional

Preparation:

Make copies or a transparency of the "What Would You Like to Play?" page.

Suggested procedure:

Ask each student to choose an instrument that he or she has dreamed of playing. Practice the solo with various instrument choices. Help students alter the rhythm of the solo to accommodate instrument names. Choose a soloist. The class sings the song, asking the question, "What would you like to play?" The soloist responds singing about his or her "dream instrument." Either the soloist or the leader may select another soloist and the song is repeated.

Other ideas:

1. Add a class response after each solo, using the same melody as the solo line. "He'd (or she'd) like to play a _____."
2. Use this game song to reinforce work with orchestral instruments and their families. Use the lyrics to illustrate the four basic families of orchestral instruments. (A representative member of each family is named.) Specify on a given day that each "dream" instrument must be a member of a particular family (string, woodwind, brass, percussion).
3. Write the names of instrument families on the board. Divide the class into instrument family groups. Begin singing the song as you point to the name of one family group. The featured group stands and each member sings about one instrument. Continue repeating the last four measures of the song until each group member has sung a solo. Then select another family name, and start the song again.
4. Use instruments not commonly found in an orchestra to create a special version of the song.

What Would You Like to Play?

(2—32)

Class:

Choose a snare drum or a flute, or a trum-pet you can toot.

What would you like to play? May-be cel-lo is your thing Cuz___

you pre-fer a string. What would you like to play? Solo: I'd like to play a (tuba).

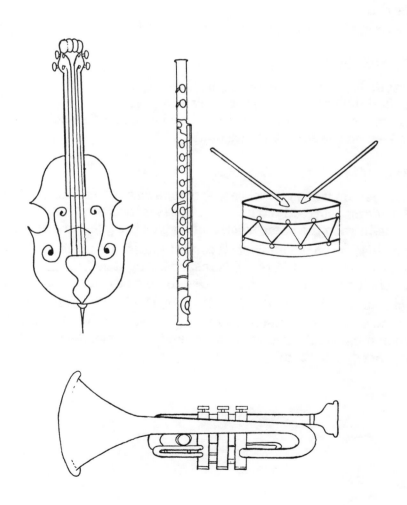

Who Has the Button?

Pitch content: dmff#s

Predominant pitch(es)/pattern(s): sfmd

Suggested grade level(s): 4 and 5

Formation: Circle

Materials required:
- "Who Has the Button?" page (master 2–33)
- disk (master 2–4), page 40, or a button

Preparation:
1. If the disk is used, make a copy of the master and cut out the disk. Color the disk and laminate for longer wear. Glue it onto heavy paper or a plastic coffee can lid.
2. Make copies or a transparency of the "Who Has the Button?" page.

Suggested procedure:

Choose one student to be "It." He or she sits in a chair, facing away from the class. The class, seated in a circle, sings the song and passes the button (or disk) from person to person, behind their backs. The person who is "It" tries to guess who has the button, based on the soloist's voice quality.

Other ideas:
1. Let the person who is "It" choose someone else to take his or her place if he or she guesses correctly. If he or she guesses incorrectly, the class sings the song again with the same soloist, and gives the guesser another try.
2. Add a class response after each correct guess, a musical affirmation that the guess was correct. A possible response might be "_____ has the button behind her (or his) back." Use the melody in measures 9 and 10.
3. Encourage vocal improvisation. Require that all conversation during the game be sung. The person who is "It" must sing his or her guesses, the teacher must sing all instructions, and class members must sing their comments or questions.

94

Who Has the Button?

(2—33)

Class:

1 2
Ack - a - lack - a Tack - a - lack - a Jer - e - mi - ah Joe,

3 4
Ev - 'ry - bod - y's voice sounds dif - f'rent you know.

5 6
Ack - a - lack - a Tack - a - lack - a Min - ne - sot - ta Mack,

7 8
Who has the but - ton be - hind_____ your back?

Solo:
9 10
I have the but - ton be - nind_____ my back.

Songs for General Use

Conversation Game

Pitch content: ms

Predominant pitch(es)/pattern(s): sm

Suggested grade level(s): 1 to 4

Formation: Teacher's choice

Materials required:

- "Conversation Game" page (master 2–34)
- conversation prompt cards (master 2–35)
- disk (master 2–4), page 40.

Preparation:

1. Make a copy of the conversation prompt cards. Color the cards and laminate them for longer use. Cut the cards apart.
2. Make a copy of the disk pattern and cut out the disk. Color the disk and laminate for longer wear. Glue it onto heavy paper or a plastic coffee can lid.
3. Make copies or a transparency of the "Conversation Game" page.

Suggested procedure:

Select three questions from the prompt cards. Sing one question as students pass the disk from person to person. The student holding the disk at the end of the question will sing the answer.

Other ideas:

1. Simplify the task by using only one question. Practice several possible options so that all students are comfortable with at least one response before you begin.
2. Add questions according to students' ability. Change the questions during the game.
3. Ask a student to take your place as the leader.

4. Change the melody of the questions. When students can match and respond to the original pattern, change to a more difficult pattern. Change again to reinforce work that you are doing on a specific interval or melodic pattern. You might eventually use this game with a variety of questions and a random order of melodic patterns for an excellent ear-training exercise.

5. Show students how to improvise new melodies to answer questions musically. Point out the differences between exact matching and answering musical questions with consequent phrases.

Conversation Game

Leader:

Do you ride a bus to school?

Solo:

(Yes, I ride on bus e - lev'n.)
(No, I don't, I walk to school.)

2. What is your middle name?
3. Do you have a dog or cat?
4. What's your fav'rite color?
5. What is your teacher's name?
6. Can you tell us your address?

Do you ride a bus to school?	What's your favorite color?
Who is your teacher?	Can you tell us your address?
Do you have a dog or cat?	What is your middle name?
What's your favorite class in school?	What is your phone number?

The Cowhand

Pitch content: s,t,drmfs

Predominant pitch(es)/pattern(s): sfmrd s, dmsfr

Suggested grade level(s): K to 3

Formation: Teacher's choice

Materials required:
- "The Cowhand" page (master 2–36)
- cowhand pictures, optional (masters 2–37 and 2–38)

Preparation:
1. Duplicate the cowhand pictures. Color them and laminate for longer wear. Cut the pictures apart.
2. Make copies or a transparency of "The Cowhand" page.

Suggested procedure:

Help the class sing measures 1 through 8. Select a soloist to sing measures 9 and 10 and name something that a cowhand might need (such as a horse, lasso, boots, hat, saddle, guitar, spurs). Repeat the song as the soloist chooses another student to sing the next solo.

Other ideas:
1. Display three cowhand pictures to simplify the decision-making process for very young children.
2. Make the game more difficult. Require each new soloist to think of something that has not been named previously.
3. Make the song cumulative by "saving solos." For example, soloist #1 sings "She would like a horse." The song is repeated. Soloist #2 sings "She would like a lasso," and soloist #1 sings again, "She would like a horse." After the third repetition of the song, three soloists sing, etc.

(2–36)

The Cowhand

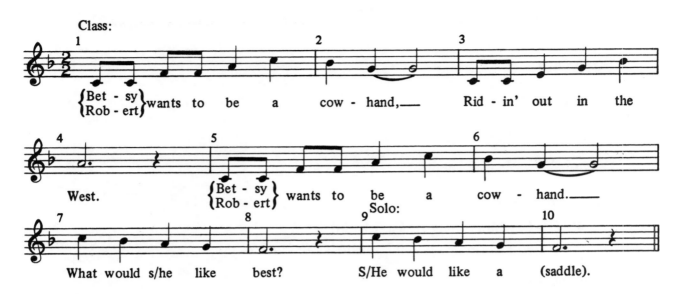

Class:

{Bet - sy / Rob - ert} wants to be a cow - hand,___ Rid - in' out in the

West.   {Bet - sy / Rob - ert} wants to be a cow - hand.___

What would s/he like best?   Solo: S/He would like a (saddle).

HORSE

GUITAR

LASSO

SADDLE

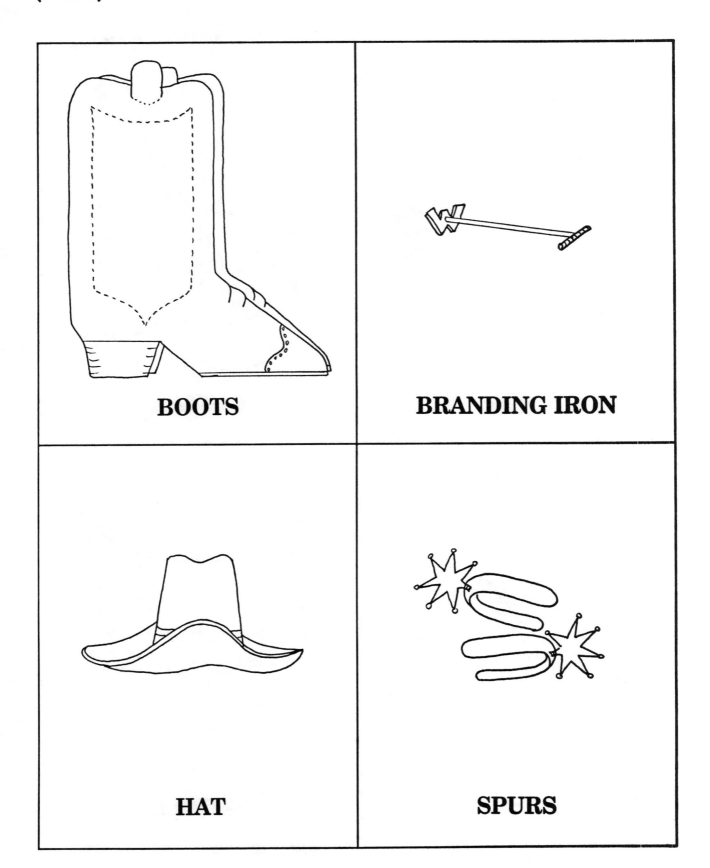

BOOTS

BRANDING IRON

HAT

SPURS

Fill the Basket

Pitch content: drmsl

Predominant pitch(es)/pattern(s): rsd

Suggested grade level(s): K to 3

Formation: Circle with a basket in the center

Materials required:

- "Fill the Basket" page (master 2–39)
- fruit pictures (master 2–40 and 2–41)
- basket

Preparation:

1. Duplicate the fruit pictures. Color them and laminate for longer wear. Cut the pictures apart.
2. Make copies or a transparency of the "Fill the Basket" page.

Suggested procedure:

Distribute the fruit pictures so that each child has one item. Children lay their fruits on the floor in front of them, and clap the beat while they sing measures 1 through 8. The leader begins the questions with "Who has a peach?" Children respond in small groups, all peaches singing together, all pears, etc. As each small group sings, the children come forward and place their fruits in the basket. Repeat the song after two question/answer sequences. Continue with other fruits (orange, plum, cherries, apple, banana, grapes). When all fruits are in the basket, redistribute them and repeat the entire song.

Other ideas:

1. Add movement. Instruct students to step the beat of the song and move around the circle while singing measures 1 through 8. Movement should stop for the question/answer portion of the song.
2. Place all fruits on the floor in a circle. As the class sings measures 1 through 8, they step the beat on the outer edge of the fruit circle. Each child stops by one fruit when the questions begin.
3. Sing the optional ending when all fruits are in the basket, and tip them out onto the floor.
4. Use items other than fruit, such as numbers, vowels, consonants, music symbols, etc.

105

Fill the Basket

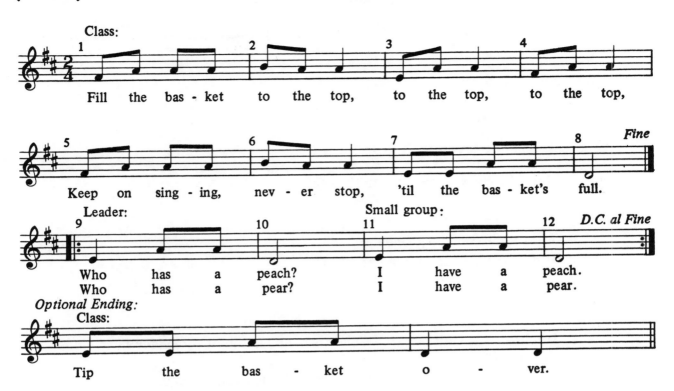

Fill the bas - ket to the top, to the top, to the top,

Keep on sing - ing, nev - er stop, 'til the bas - ket's full.

Who has a peach? I have a peach.
Who has a pear? I have a pear.

Optional Ending:

Tip the bas - ket o - ver.

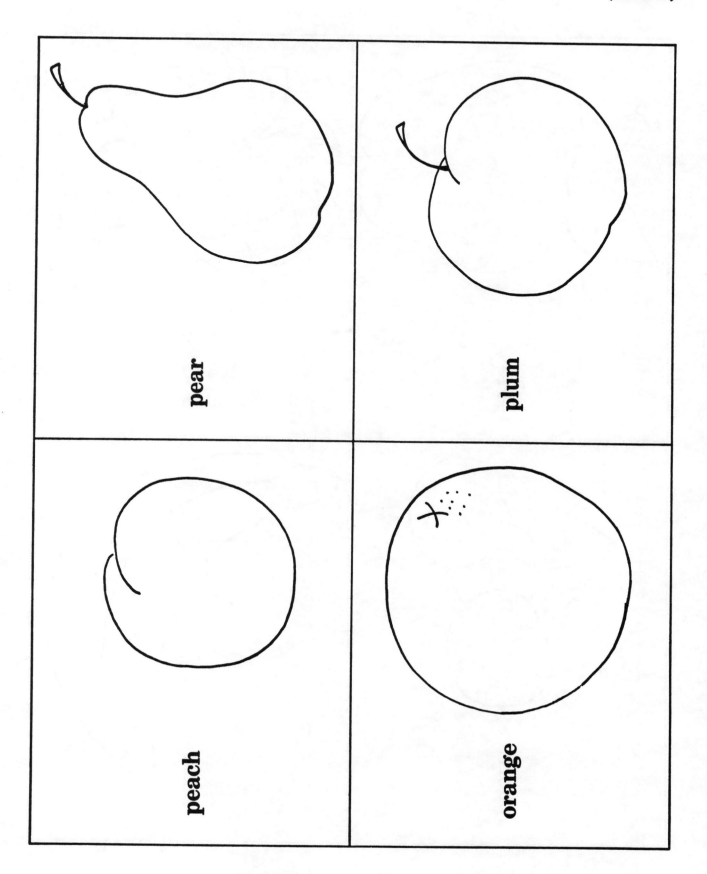

Going Out to Lunch

Pitch content: drmfsl

Predominant pitch(es)/pattern(s): smd

Suggested grade level(s): K to 3

Formation: Teacher's choice

Materials required:

- "Going Out to Lunch" page (master 2–42)
- blank cards, optional
- hat, optional

Preparation:

Make copies or a transparency of the "Going Out to Lunch" page.

Suggested procedure:

Help the class sing measures 1 through 4. Select a soloist to sing measures 5 and 6 and name his or her favorite restaurant. The soloist selects the next soloist, and the song is repeated. Alter the rhythm of measures 5 and 6 to accommodate the names of some restaurants.

Other ideas:

1. Let your class choose several favorite restaurants. Print the name of each on a card, and place cards in a hat. Choose a student to draw a card as the class sings measures 1 through 6. All students who like the selected restaurant will sing the solo part together as a small group.
2. Have students invent names of restaurants, and sing about their own restaurants as solos.

(2—42)

Going Out to Lunch

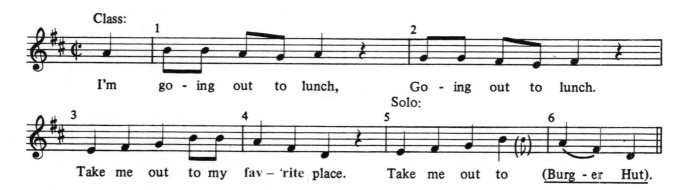

Class:

I'm go - ing out to lunch, Go - ing out to lunch.

Solo:

Take me out to my fav – 'rite place. Take me out to (Burg - er Hut).

Going to the Zoo

Pitch content: drmfsl

Predominant pitch(es)/pattern(s): sfmrd

Suggested grade level(s): K to 2

Formation: Teacher's choice

Materials required:
- "Going to the Zoo" page (master 2–43)
- zoo pictures, optional (masters 2–44 and 2–45)

Preparation:
1. If the zoo pictures are used, make copies of the masters. Color the pictures and then laminate for longer wear. Cut the pictures apart.
2. Make copies or a transparency of the "Going to the Zoo" page.

Suggested procedure:

Choose a soloist. The class sings measures 1 through 8. The soloist sings measures 9 and 10, and chooses another soloist. Repeat the song.

Other ideas:
1. Display pictures of the zoo animals. Use only three pictures at a time to simplify the decision-making process for very young children.
2. Add movement. Help students clap, tap knees, or step the beat as they sing. Movement should stop during the solos.
3. Change the lyrics to "We're going to the farm." The third phrase could be "Cows and chicks and a bumblebee."
4. Change the lyrics to "We're going to the store." The third phrase and fourth phrase could be "Eggs and milk and an apple pie, Tell us what we'll buy."
5. Add a class response after each solo. Class members can echo the solo part exactly.

(2—43) # Going to the Zoo

Pitch content: drmfsld'

Predominant pitch(es)/pattern(s): dd' d'd repeated s

Suggested grade level(s): 1 and 2

Formation: Teacher's choice

Materials required:

- "Helicopter Pilot" page (master 2–46)
- beanbag, optional
- resonator bells, optional

Preparation:

Make copies or a transparency of the "Helicopter Pilot" page.

Suggested procedure:

Choose one soloist to sing all solo parts, or three children, one for each solo part. Repeat the song with new soloists.

Other ideas:

1. Form a circle with the soloist in the center. Class members join hands, circle around the soloist, and sing measures 1 through 8. Movement stops at measure 9. Class members sing measures 9, 11, and 13, and create movement to match the melodic movement. The soloist echoes and mirrors the class.
2. Select a student to stand in the center of the circle. He or she chooses a soloist by tossing a beanbag to a classmate. The soloist sings all three solos, and becomes the new "tosser" as the song begins again.
3. Add resonator bells to the solo parts.

(2—46)   # Helicopter Pilot

Class:
1   2   3   4
Hel - i - cop - ter   pi - lot   yes,   that's   me.

5   6   7   8   *Fine*
I   can   fly   a   chop - per,   wait   and   see.

Solo: Class: Solo:
9   10   11   12
Go - ing   up.   Go - ing   up.   Go - ing   down.   Go - ing   down.

Class:
13   14   15   16   *D.C. al Fine*
Hov - er   in   the   mid - dle.   Hov - er   in   the   mid - dle.

The Helpers in Our School

Pitch content: drmsl

Predominant pitch(es)/pattern(s): mrsd   smlsm

Suggested grade level(s): K and 1

Formation: Teacher's choice

Materials required:

- "The Helpers in Our School" page (master 2–47)
- school helper pictures, optional (master 2–48)

Preparation:

1. If the school helper pictures are used, duplicate the master. Color the pictures and laminate them for longer wear. Cut the pictures apart.
2. Make copies or a transparency of "The Helpers in Our School" page.

Suggested procedure:

Help the class sing measures 1 through 8. Hold up a picture of a cook and sing "The cook is Mrs. (Mr.) _____." The class echoes. Repeat the song as many times as desired. Sing about other school helpers, such as principal, secretary, librarian, janitor, bus driver.

Other ideas:

1. Follow the suggested procedure, omitting the pictures.
2. Select any one student to sing the echo.
3. Instruct students to raise their hands to volunteer for a solo. The class sings measures 1 through 8. The soloist sings measures 9 to 11. The class echoes the soloist.
4. Simplify the solo-response section by eliminating either names or titles. Sing (on sol mi) "The cook," echo: "The Cook," or "Mr. Carlson," echo: "Mr. Carlson."
5. Change the lyrics to ". . .the helpers in our town." Help your students name "firefighters, police officers, doctors, mail carriers," etc.
6. Change the lyrics to ". . .the helpers in our class." Help your students name "milk helper, errand runner, housekeeper," etc.

(2—47)   # The Helpers in Our School

Class:
Who are the help - ers, the help - ers in our school?

Who are the help - ers, the help - ers in our school?

Leader:
The cook is (Mrs. An - der - son).

Class:
The cook is (Mrs. An - der - son).

Hot Dogs and Buns

Pitch content: drmfsl

Predominant pitch(es)/pattern(s): slls

Suggested grade level(s): 1 to 3

Formation: Teacher's choice

Materials required:
- "Hot Dogs and Buns" page (master 2–49)
- hot dog spinner, optional (master 2–50)
- disk, optional (master 2–4), page 40.

Preparation:
1. If the disk is used, make a copy of the master and cut out the disk. Color it and laminate it for longer wear. Glue the disk onto heavy paper or a plastic coffee can lid.
2. If the hot dog spinner is used, make a copy of the master. Glue it onto heavy paper, and cut out the spinner and pointer. Attach the pointer to the center of the spinner with a brass fastener.
3. Make copies or a transparency of the "Hot Dogs and Buns" page.

Suggested procedure:

Instruct each child to prepare a solo, indicating what he or she would like on top of a hot dog. Help the class sing measures 1 through 4. Sing measure 5 as a solo. Select a student to sing measure 6 as a solo. Help the class respond with measures 7 and 8, and repeat the song. Use a different soloist each time for measure 6.

Other ideas:
1. Use the disk to select a new soloist. Pass the disk from person to person. The child holding the disk at measure 5 is the soloist for measure 6.
2. Make the song cumulative by "saving solos." For example, soloist #1 stands and sings "Ketchup on mine." The song is repeated. Soloist #2 stands and sings "Mustard on mine," and soloist #1 (still standing) sings again "Ketchup on mine." After the third repetition of the song, three soloists sing, etc.

120

3. Spin the hot dog spinner to determine the lucky topping after five (or more) children are standing. The child(ren) who sang the lucky topping will spin the spinner for the next game.

4. Allow every child a chance to sing a solo. Take turns going around the classroom. Use this method with or without the cumulative ending.

(2–49)　　　　**Hot Dogs and Buns**

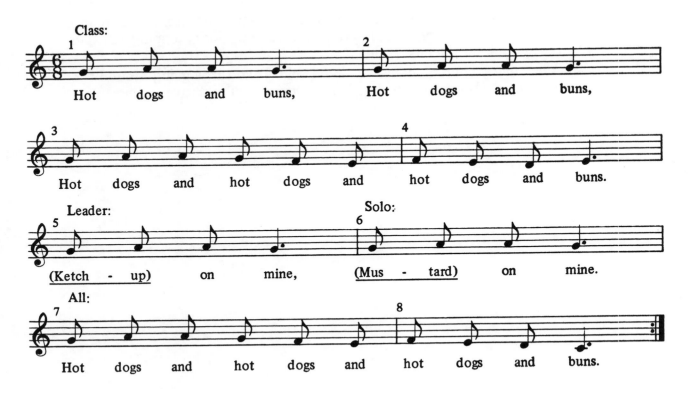

Class:

Hot　dogs　and　buns,　Hot　dogs　and　buns,

Hot　dogs　and　hot　dogs　and　hot　dogs　and　buns.

Leader:　　　　　　　　　　　Solo:

(Ketch - up)　on　mine,　(Mus - tard)　on　mine.

All:

Hot　dogs　and　hot　dogs　and　hot　dogs　and　buns.

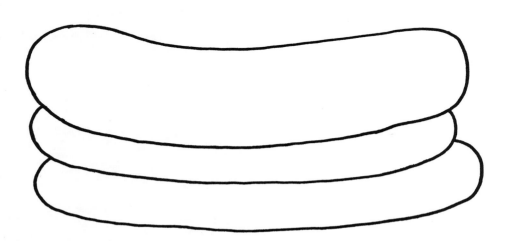

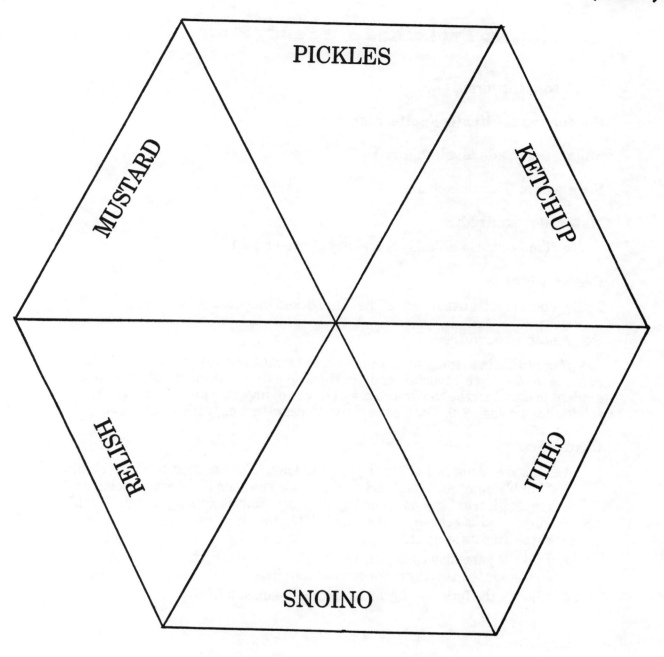

PICKLES

MUSTARD

KETCHUP

RELISH

CHILI

SNOINO

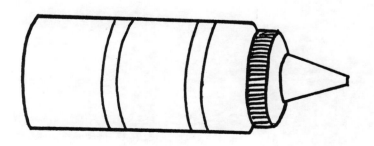

I'm Locked in a Candy Store

Pitch content: drmsl

Predominant pitch(es)/pattern(s): ls

Suggested grade level(s): 1 to 3

Formation: Teacher's choice

Materials required:

- "I'm Locked in a Candy Store" page (master 2–51)

Preparation:

Make copies or a transparency of the "I'm Locked in a Candy Store" page.

Suggested procedure:

Ask your students to imagine the fun of being locked in a candy store. Help them prepare to sing their favorite candy in the solo pattern (measure 9). Choose one student to stand and be the first soloist. The class sings measures 1 through 8. The soloist sings measure 9. The class echoes. Repeat the song with a new soloist.

Other ideas:

1. Make the song cumulative by "saving solos." For example, soloist #1 sings "Bubble gum" and is echoed by the class. The song is repeated. Soloist #2 sings "Licorice" and is echoed by the class. Soloist #1 sings again "Bubble gum," and is echoed by the class. After the third repetition of the song, three soloists sing, etc.
2. Play the game in a circle, with each soloist standing. The order for choosing soloists is the seating order around the circle.
3. Change the lyrics to "toy store" or "ice cream store."

124

I'm Locked in a Candy Store

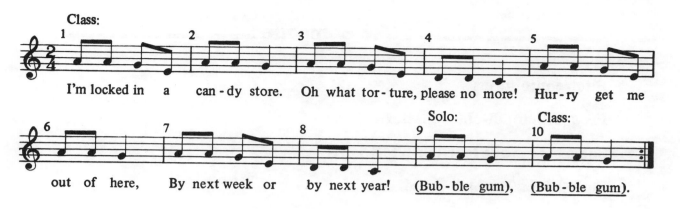

Class:

1 2 3 4 5

I'm locked in a can-dy store. Oh what tor-ture, please no more! Hur-ry get me

6 7 8 Solo: Class:
9 10

out of here, By next week or by next year! (Bub-ble gum), (Bub-ble gum).

PEPPERMINTS   Jelly Beans   Gum Drops

I See Someone

Pitch content: ms

Predominant pitch(es)/pattern(s): sm

Suggested grade level(s): K to 2

Formation: Teacher's choice

Materials required:

- "I See Someone" page (master 2–52)

Preparation:

Make copies or a transparency of the "I See Someone" page.

Suggested procedure:

Select a mystery person and sing measures 1 through 4. Students raise their hands to guess the identity of the mystery person. Select a guesser who sings measures 5 and 6 as a solo. Respond with measures 7 and 8. If the guesser is correct, begin the song again, and sing about a new mystery person. If the guesser is wrong, select another guesser, and repeat measures 5 through 8 until a correct guess is made.

Other ideas:

1. Announce the color that the mystery person is wearing, and have the entire class sing the song with you.
2. Allow a correct guesser to help you select the next mystery person. Sing measures 1 through 4 and 7 and 8 with the student. Allow him or her to select the guessers.
3. Allow a correct guesser to become the new leader, and sing measures 1 through 4 and 7 and 8 alone.
4. Choose one child to be "It." He or she goes out of the room. The class chooses a mystery person and agrees on the color of that student's clothing. "It" comes back into the room. The whole class sings the song. "It" sings the solo (measures 5 and 6) and guesses the mystery person's identity. The class sings measures 7 and 8.

126

I See Someone

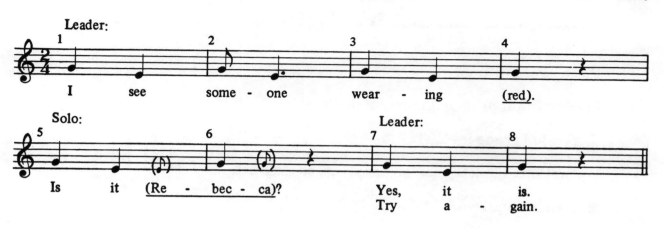

Leader: I see some-one wear-ing (red).

Solo: Is it (Re-bec-ca)?

Leader: Yes, it is. / Try a-gain.

It's Magic!

Pitch content: drmfsl

Predominant pitch(es)/pattern(s): sfmrd

Suggested grade level(s): 2 to 4

Formation: Black top hat (prepared box) on table in front of class

Materials required:
- "It's Magic!" page (master 2–53)
- hat (master 2–54)
- magic items (master 2–55 and master 2–56)
- shallow box
- black top hat, optional
- white gloves
- resonator bells, optional
- piano, optional

Preparation:
1. Make a copy of the hat. Color it and laminate for longer use. Cut out the hat and attach it to the side of the shallow box.
2. Make a copy of the magic items. Color the pictures and laminate them for longer use. Cut the cards apart and place them inside the shallow box.
3. Make copies or a transparency of the "It's Magic!" page.

Suggested procedure:

Place duplicated magic items inside the decorated shallow box. Select three students to be magicians, and show them the contents of the magic box. Give a pair of white gloves to magician #1. The class sings measures 1 through 10. The magician sings the solo measures 11 and 12, naming an item he or she will pull from the hat. That student then gives the gloves to magician #2, and the song is repeated.

128

Other ideas:

1. Place actual magic novelties inside a real black top hat.
2. Use the optional interlude. Help the class sing "Tahdah" after the magician's solos. Choose an announcer to speak the introduction. Magician #1 reaches into the hat and pulls out the named item. The class responds with another "Tahdah" and, of course, applause and cheers. The gloves are given to magician #2 and the song and magic show are repeated.
3. Add a drum roll, created by the audience with their fingers and knees.
4. Add resonator bells to the "Tahdah."
5. Add piano chords to the "Tahdah."

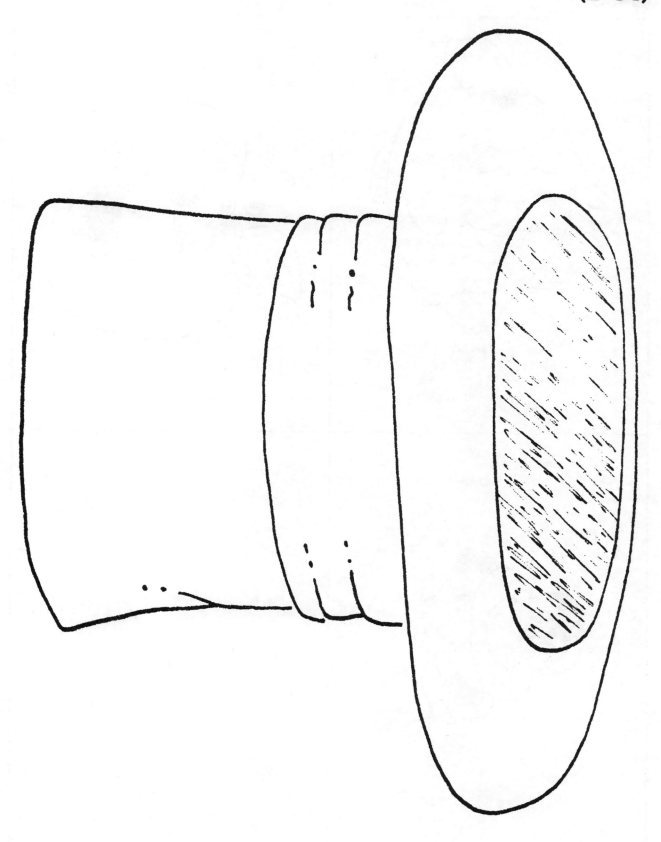

(2–55)

Lucky Numbers

Pitch content: dms

Predominant pitch(es)/pattern(s): sm

Suggested grade level(s): K to 3

Formation: Number cards and spinner arranged on the floor in the center of a circle

Materials required:
- "Lucky Numbers" page (master 2–57)
- spinner (master 2–58)
- number cards (masters 2–59 through 2–64)
- die, optional
- hat, optional
- musical die, optional
- prizes, optional

Preparation:
1. Duplicate the number cards, using colored paper if possible. Glue the cards to heavy paper and laminate for longer wear.
2. Duplicate the spinner master and glue to heavy paper. Cut out the spinner and pointer. Attach the pointer to the center of the spinner with a brass fastener.
3. Make copies or a transparency of the "Lucky Numbers" page.

Suggested procedure:

Students will spin the pointer, step, and stand on number cards. Select one student to spin the pointer. He or she will step on the cards, advancing as far as the indicated number. For example, if the student spins 5, he or she advances to card number 5. The class sings the song as the player advances. The player stops, stands on a card, and waits for another student to have a turn. Subsequent players follow the same procedure. If a student spins the number of an occupied card, the class sings "and bump," instead of "and stop." The original player must sit down, and is replaced by the new player. When all six cards are occupied, the leader spins the pointer. The lucky number is called out, and the winner becomes the lucky number spinner for the next game.

Other ideas:

1. Replace the spinner by shaking dice or drawing numbers from a hat.
2. Use a musical die instead of the spinner. Make a cube of wood, foam rubber, or cardboard. Paint a note or rest value on each side of the cube.
3. Allow the winner to select a prize in addition to being the spinner for the next game.

(2–57) **Lucky Numbers**

© 2003 Heritage Music Press, a division of The Lorenz Corporation

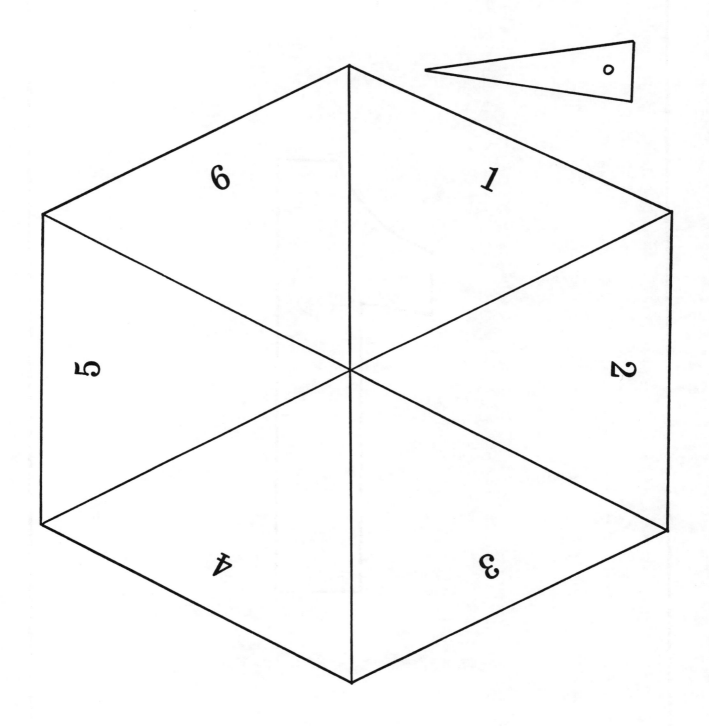

(2–61)

Pitch content: l,t,drmff#ss#1

Predominant pitch(es)/pattern(s): mf#s#1

Suggested grade level(s): K to 2

Formation: Bridge built from two chairs; children on one side of bridge, troll underneath

Materials required:
- "Mister Troll" page (master 2–65)
- two chairs

Preparation:
Make copies or a transparency of the "Mister Troll" page.

Suggested procedure:
Select one student to be the troll. The class sings measures 1 through 12. The troll sings measures 13 and 14 as a solo, and specifies the color of clothing the children must wear in order to cross the bridge. Eligible children sing measures 15 and 16 and then cross the bridge. They wait on the other side. Repeat the song with other colors until all children have crossed the bridge.

Other ideas:
1. Change the lyrics of measures 13 and 14 to another specification for crossing the bridge. For example, "If your name is _____ ," answer with "My name is _____ ."
2. Correlate with the story of "The Three Billy Goats Gruff."
3. Allow children to dramatize the story and improvise melodies for the dialogue.

144

Mister Troll

Class:
Mis - ter Troll, Mis - ter Troll, May we cross your bridge?

Mis - ter Troll, Mis - ter Troll, May we cross your bridge?

Let us pass to eat some grass. May we cross your bridge?

Solo:
If you're wear - ing (yellow).

Small group:
I am wear - ing (yellow).

The Monster Game

Pitch content: ms

Predominant pitch(es)/pattern(s): sm

Suggested grade level(s): K to 2

Formation: Teacher's choice

Materials required:
- "The Monster Game" page (master 2–66)
- monster cards (masters 2–67 through 2–71)
- paper bag

Preparation:
1. Make copies of the monster cards, allowing 5 to 8 cards per student. Color the pictures and laminate them for longer wear. Cut the cards apart.
2. Make copies or a transparency of "The Monster Game" page.

Suggested procedure:

Place the monster cards in a paper bag. Sing a request (similar to measure 1), standing near or signaling any child in the class. The child responds; for example, "I'll sing red." Allow the soloist to draw a monster card from the bag. Continue with another request directed to another student. Each student attempts to create a complete monster by earning four cards: (1) a head, (2) arms, (3) a tummy, and (4) feet. The fun begins when children assemble strange combinations of body parts.

Other ideas:
1. Seat students at desks or tables.
2. Invent more requests (for example, seasons, towns/cities, pizza toppings, candy bars, holidays).
3. Extend the tonal memory by using longer requests that require longer answers. See "The Conversation Game" for question/answer suggestions.
4. Allow the winner (the first child to build a complete monster) to help you distribute monster cards for the next game.
5. Allow the winner to sing the requests for the next game.

146

The Monster Game

(2—66)

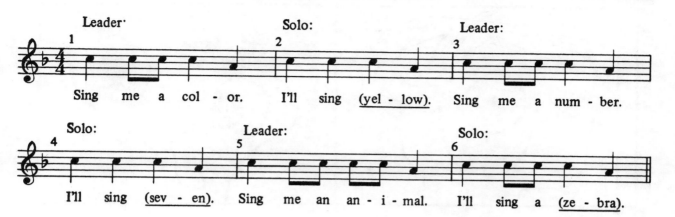

Sing me a col - or. I'll sing (yel - low). Sing me a num - ber.

I'll sing (sev - en). Sing me an an - i - mal. I'll sing a (ze - bra).

(2–67)

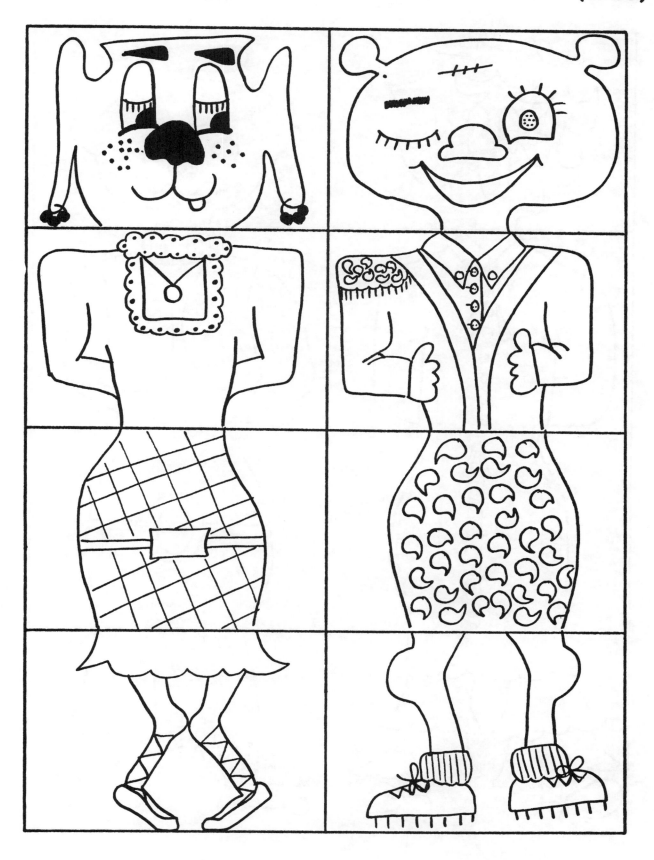

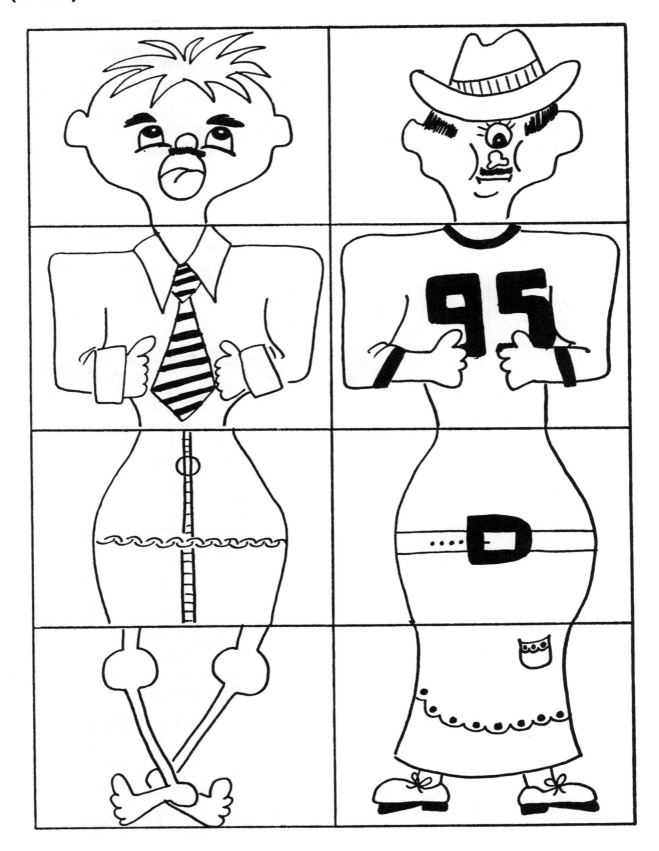

Pitch content: drmsl

Predominant pitch(es)/pattern(s): sm

Suggested grade level(s): 2 and 3

Formation: Teacher's choice

Materials required:
- "Mountain Man" page (master 2–72)
- Mountain Man costume, optional (master 2–73)
- chair or table

Preparation:
1. Enlarge the Mountain Man costume to children's full size, using a sheet of heavy paper and an opaque projector. Color the costume and laminate it for longer use. Cut out the eye and nose area.
2. Make copies or a transparency of the "Mountain Man" page.

Suggested procedure:

Select a student (boy or girl) to go up to an imaginary mountain (a chair or table top). The class sings the song except for measures 10 and 12. The soloist echoes the class in those measures, and chooses a new soloist. The song is repeated.

Other ideas:
1. Use the Mountain Man costume instead of a chair or table.
2. Select three students to hide behind a piece of classroom furniture. They decide secretly who will sing the echoes. Other class members guess whose voice they heard.
3. Try improvised musical conversation between you and members of the class as they guess the name of the soloist.
4. Give the soloist a name. For example, you could use "Mountain Dan" or "Mountain Fran."

(2–72)

Mountain Man

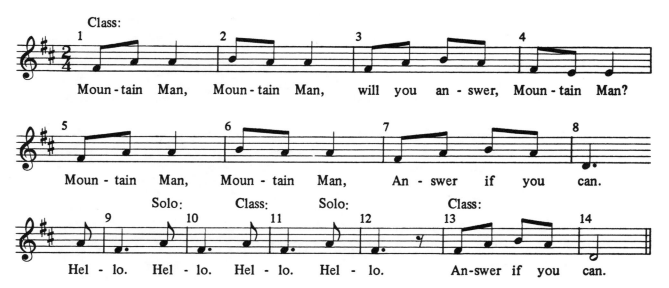

Class:

1 2 3 4

Moun - tain Man, Moun - tain Man, will you an - swer, Moun - tain Man?

5 6 7 8

Moun - tain Man, Moun - tain Man, An - swer if you can.

Solo: Class: Solo: Class:

9 10 11 12 13 14

Hel - lo. Hel - lo. Hel - lo. Hel - lo. An-swer if you can.

Pitch content: dmsl

Predominant pitch(es)/pattern(s): slsmd

Suggested grade level(s): 1 to 4

Formation: Teacher's choice

Materials required:
- "Musical Math" page (master 2–74)
- number cards (masters 2–75 and 2–76)

Preparation:
1. Make copies of the number cards. Color the cards and laminate them for longer wear. Cut the cards apart.
2. Make copies or a transparency of the "Musical Math" page.

Suggested procedure:

Distribute two number cards to each student. Instruct the students to study their cards and add them together. Practice the solo with several sample pairs of cards. To begin the game, sing the first phrase. Members of the class take turns showing their cards and singing the second phrase. Use only addition until students get accustomed to calculating and singing solos.

Other ideas:
1. Instruct students to exchange one or both number cards. Sing the song as many times as necessary to allow every child to sing a solo with new members.
2. Try subtraction. Remind students to check their cards and subtract the smaller number from the larger.
3. Try using both versions, alternating between addition and subtraction.
4. Distribute blank cards. Let students fill in their own numbers, sing their solos, and then exchange cards.
5. Coordinate with the math teacher. Use addition and subtraction problems of appropriate difficulty for each grade level.

Musical Math

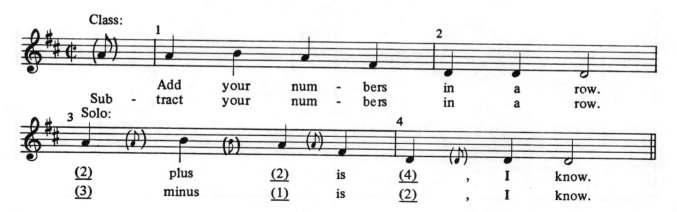

Class:

Add   your   num - bers   in   a   row.
Sub - tract   your   num - bers   in   a   row.

Solo:

(2)   plus   (2)   is   (4)   ,   I   know.
(3)   minus   (1)   is   (2)   ,   I   know.

zero 0		one 1 🍎	
two 2 🍎🍎		three 3 🍎🍎🍎	
four 4 🍎🍎🍎🍎		five 5 🍎🍎🍎🍎🍎	
six 6 🍎🍎🍎🍎🍎 🍎		seven 7 🍎🍎🍎🍎🍎 🍎🍎	

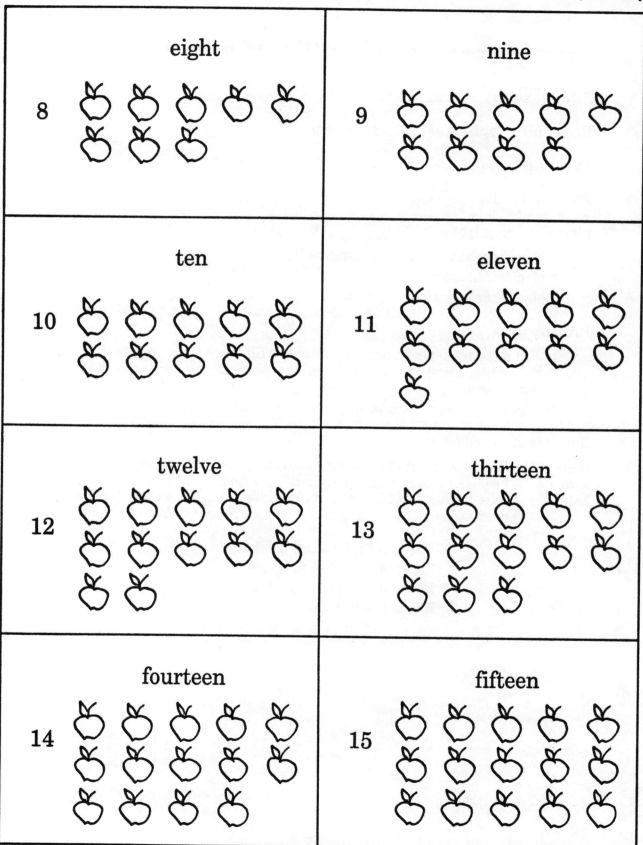

eight
8

nine
9

ten
10

eleven
11

twelve
12

thirteen
13

fourteen
14

fifteen
15

My Elephant Pat

Pitch content: s,l,t,drmfs

Predominant pitch(es)/pattern(s): sm

Suggested grade level(s): K to 2

Formation: Teacher's choice

Materials required:
- "My Elephant Pat" page (master 2–77)
- elephant (master 2–78)
- elephant clothes (master 2–79)

Preparation:
1. Enlarge the elephant and the clothes to fill large sheets of heavy paper, using the opaque projector. Color the pictures and laminate them for longer wear.
2. Make copies or a transparency of the "My Elephant Pat" page.

Suggested procedure:

Distribute the elephant clothes to five students. The class sings measures 1 through 8. The leader sings "Who has his hat?" The student holding the elephant's hat sings "I have his hat," and brings it forward. Tape the hat on the elephant as the class sings measures 11 and 12. Repeat the song for other clothes as follows:

> My Elephant Burt has lost his shirt.
> My Elephant Guy has lost his tie.
> My Elephant Brock has lost his sock.
> My Elephant Blue has lost his shoe.

160

Other ideas:

1. Add an optional ending to the song when all of the clothes have been returned.

My el - e-phant Joe is read-y to go, read-y to go, read-y to go.

My el - e-phant Joe is read-y to go. Now he's read-y to go.

2. Help students create additional verses to the song.

3. Compose a new version of the song. Try a version about toys:

> My Elephant Ted has lost his sled.
> My Elephant Gus has lost his bus.
> My Elephant Char has lost her car.
> My Elephant Mike has lost his bike.

(2–77)   # My Elephant Pat

My el-e-phant Pat has lost his hat, lost his hat, lost his hat. My

el-e-phant Pat has lost his hat. Help us find his hat.

Solo: *Class:*   *D.C. al Fine*

Who has his hat? I have his hat. Bring it back to my el-e-phant Pat.

2. My elephant Burt has lost his shirt.
3. My elephant Guy has lost his tie.
4. My elephant Brock has lost his sock.
5. My elephant Blue has lost his shoe.

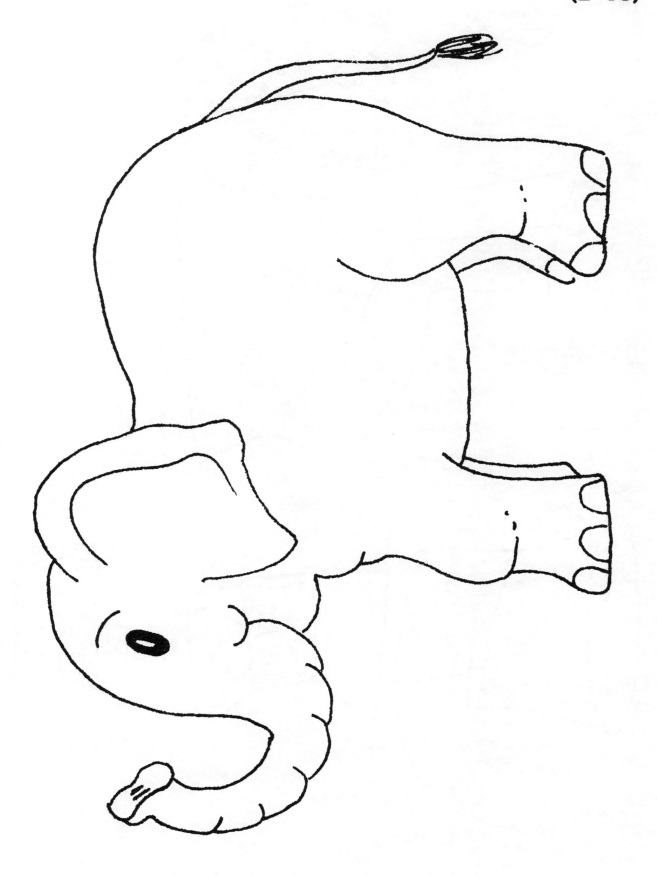

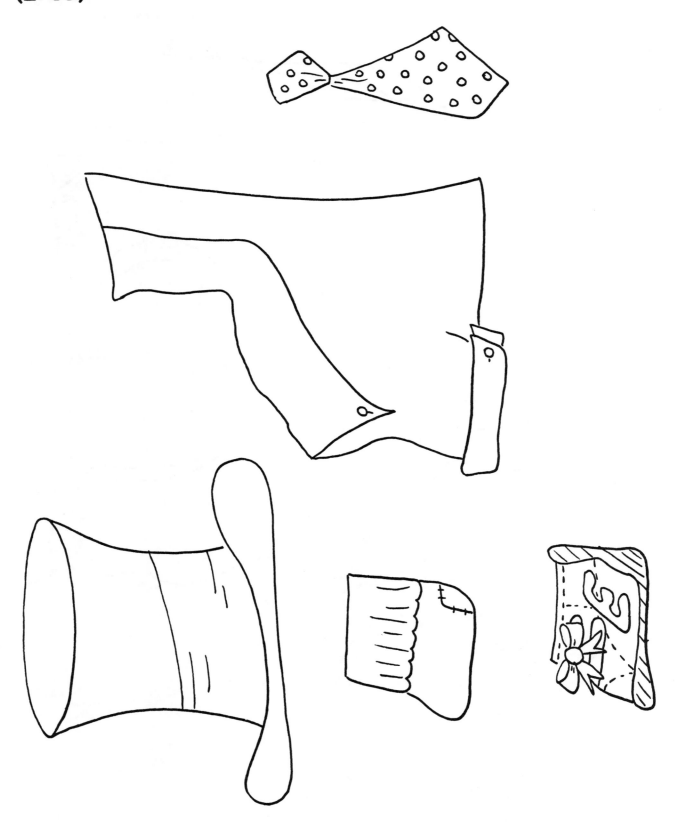

Riding on the Railroad

Pitch content: drmsl

Predominant pitch(es)/pattern(s): mrd

Suggested grade level(s): K to 3

Formation: Circle

Materials required:
- "Riding on the Railroad" page (master 2–80)
- chairs
- sand blocks and bell, optional

Preparation:

Make copies or a transparency of the "Riding on the Railroad" page.

Suggested procedure:

Have students sit in a circle. Choose one child to be the leader of the train. As the class sings measures 1 through 8, the leader of the train shuffles around the outside of the circle. At measure 8, the leader chooses the soloist by stopping behind a classmate. The soloist, after singing measure 9, joins the leader, and the class adds his or her name to the train. List children's names in reverse order (from caboose to engine), always ending with "And _____ leads the train."

Other ideas:
1. Add movement. Help class members move bent arms or clap the beat while singing.
2. Change the lyrics to sing about your city; for example, "Take the train to Boston," (or "Going to St. Louis").
3. Add sand blocks and a train bell for sound effects. Allow the leader of the train to sing or say "All aboard!" before the train departs.

(2—80)

Riding on the Railroad

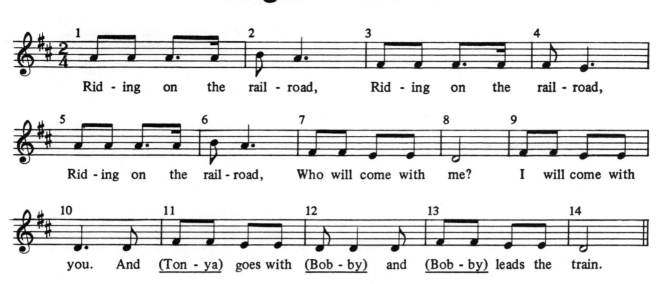

Rid - ing on the rail - road, Rid - ing on the rail - road,

Rid - ing on the rail - road, Who will come with me? I will come with

you. And (Ton - ya) goes with (Bob - by) and (Bob - by) leads the train.

Someone Has the Color

Pitch content: s,t,drms

Predominant pitch(es)/pattern(s): sm

Suggested grade level(s): K to 2

Formation: Teacher's choice

Materials required:

- "Someone Has the Color" page (master 2–81)
- color cards (master 2–82)
- color puppets, optional (masters 2–83 and 2–84)

Preparation:

1. Duplicate the color cards master. Color the cards and laminate for longer wear. Cut the cards apart.
2. Duplicate the color puppets master. Color the pictures and laminate for longer wear. Cut out the puppets and the finger holes.
3. Make copies or a transparency of the "Someone Has the Color" page.

Suggested procedure:

Distribute six color cards among the class members. Sing measure 1 about any one of the colors, such as "Who has the red?" The student holding the red card responds with measure 2. The class sings measures 3 and 4 and completes the song with a knee pat (patsch) followed by a clap. Continue the song by asking about the other colors. When all six students have sung, they give the cards to six new students. Play the game again.

Other ideas:

1. Add movement. Have class members stand whenever they sing their part and sit as soon as they finish. The quick pop-up action creates a fun movement game.
2. Use the color puppets instead of the cards.
3. Use the name of the soloist to replace the word "someone" in each class response (measures 3 and 4), such as "Betsy has the color red."
4. Use numbers and number cards instead of colors. (See the cards used in "Lucky Numbers.")
5. Use foreign words for each color, such as "Who has the *weiss*?"
6. Use music symbol cards. The class responds with "Someone has the sign for sharp."

(2—81)   **Someone Has the Color**

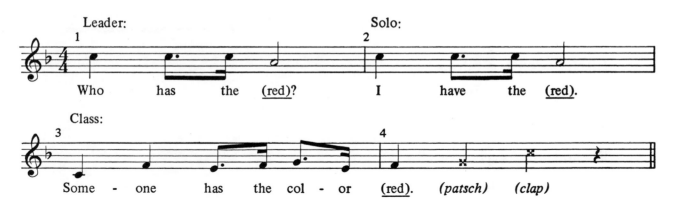

Leader: Solo:

Who has the (red)?   I have the (red).

Class:

Some - one has the col - or (red). *(patsch)* *(clap)*

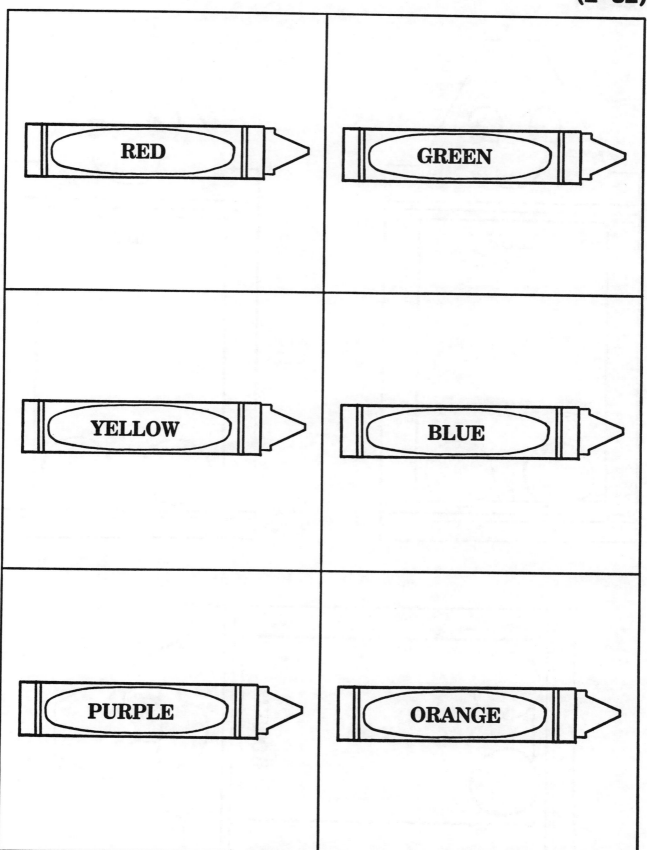

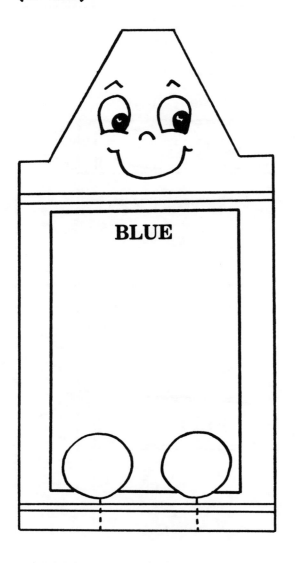

BLUE

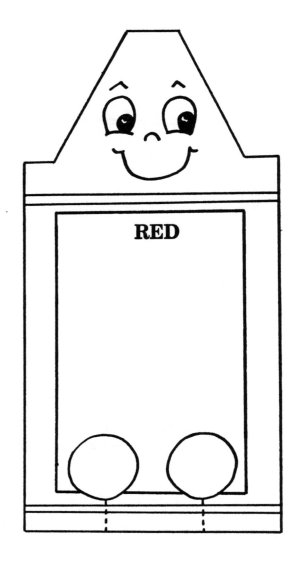

RED

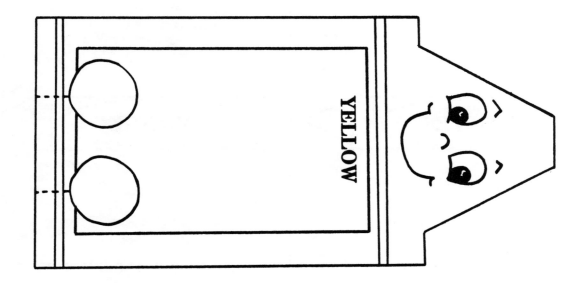

YELLOW

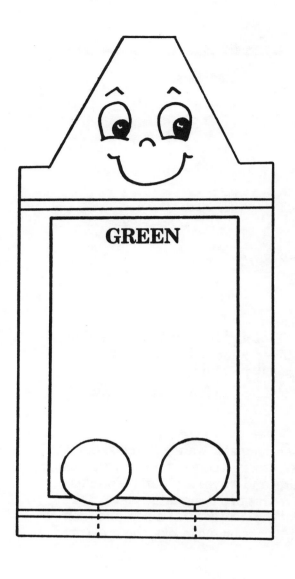

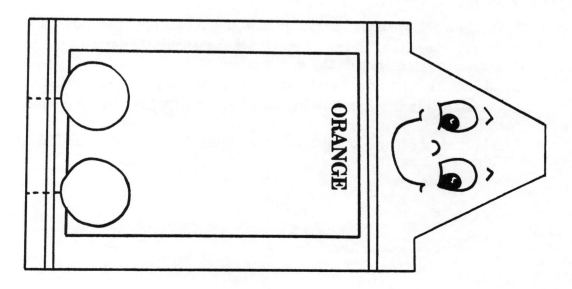

Tell Me, Tell Me, Wizard

Pitch content: msl

Predominant pitch(es)/pattern(s): ml

Suggested grade level(s): preK to 2

Formation: Teacher's choice

Materials required:

- "Tell Me, Tell Me, Wizard" page (master 2–85)
- magic wand star (master 2–86)

Preparation:

1. Duplicate the star master. Cut out the front and back pieces of the star, color them, and laminate them for longer wear. Glue the star to an unsharpened pencil or a rhythm stick to make a wand.
2. Make copies or a transparency of the "Tell Me, Tell Me, Wizard" page.

Suggested procedure:

Select a student to be the wizard. Give him or her the magic wand. The class sings measures 1 through 4 as the wizard circulates among them. The wizard sings measures 5 through 8 as a solo, names a creature, and waves the wand. The class sings measures 9 through 16, and the creature moves to a designated place in the room to get ready for the wizard's parade. Repeat the song several times, and then have a parade. Each person in the parade will walk or move like the creature they've become.

Other ideas:

1. Choose a new wizard after each parade, and repeat the entire process.
2. Sing the melody on "La La La" and clap the beat while the parade is moving around the room. Repeat the song if necessary.
3. Add a full costume for the wizard, complete with cape, hat, and wand.
4. Correlate this activity with a listening lesson on *The Sorcerer's Apprentice* by Dukas.
5. Add students' names to the song by changing the lyrics, such as "Tell me Christy Wizard. . ."

172

Tell Me, Tell Me, Wizard

Class:

Tell me, tell me, Wiz - ard, what I am?

Solo:

You are a (pup - py), Al - la ka - zaam.

Class:

Al - la ka - zaam, see what he's made.

You can be in the Wiz - ard's pa - rade.

(2—86)

Treasure Chest

Pitch content: ms

Predominant pitch(es)/pattern(s): sm

Suggested grade level(s): preK to 2

Formation: Teacher's choice

Materials required:

- "Treasure Chest" page (master 2–87)
- a treasure chest
- resonator bells, optional

Preparation:

1. Create a treasure chest from a box or covered container. Collect various small items (a penny, a ring, an eraser, a sticker, a small toy, etc.) to use for treasures. Check with the school secretary for unclaimed lost-and-found items, too.
2. Make copies or a transparency of the "Treasure Chest" page.

Suggested procedure:

Select three items from the treasure chest, and rehearse a question and answer with the class. Instruct students to close their eyes and make a "cup" out of their hands. Distribute the treasures. Sing measure 1 about one item. The child holding the treasure sings the response. The game continues for the other two items. After three soloists have responded, sing "Give them away." The three soloists get out of their places and give the items to three new soloists. The game continues.

Other ideas:

1. Use a student leader to ask the questions.
2. Vary the melody. Use different combinations of sol, mi, la, and do.
3. Add resonator bells to the question-and-answer parts. Allow students to play the bell parts.
4. Invite students to contribute treasures to the treasure chest.

(2—87) **Treasure Chest**

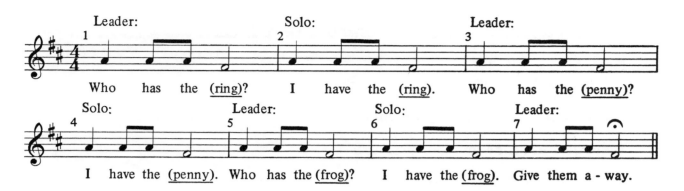

Who has the (ring)? I have the (ring). Who has the (penny)?

I have the (penny). Who has the (frog)? I have the (frog). Give them a - way.

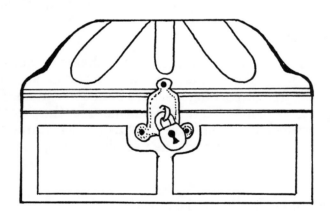

Tutti Frutti Ice Cream

Pitch content: msl

Predominant pitch(es)/pattern(s): smls

Suggested grade level(s): 1 to 3

Formation: Teacher's choice

Materials required:

- "Tutti Frutti Ice Cream" page (master 2–88)
- ice cream cone, optional (master 2–89)

Preparation:

1. Make a copy of the cone master. Color the picture and laminate it for longer wear. Cut out the ice cream cone.
2. Make copies or a transparency of the "Tutti Frutti Ice Cream" page.

Suggested procedure:

Help the class sing measures 1 through 8. While they are singing, select one child to stand and sing the solo. Repeat the song with a new soloist.

Other ideas:

1. Make the song cumulative by "saving solos." For example, soloist #1 sings "Choc'late for me." The song is repeated. Soloist #2 sings "Maple nut for me," and soloist #1 sings again "Choc'late for me." After the third repetition of the song, three soloists sing, etc.
2. Allow every child a chance to sing a solo. Take turns going around the classroom. Use this method with or without the cumulative ending.
3. Seat students in a circle. As they sing, they pass an ice cream cone (master 2–89) from person to person. The student holding the cone when it is time for a solo sings his or her favorite flavor.
4. Use idea #3 in classroom formation.
5. See "Tutti Frutti Monsters."

(2–88)

Tutti Frutti Ice Cream

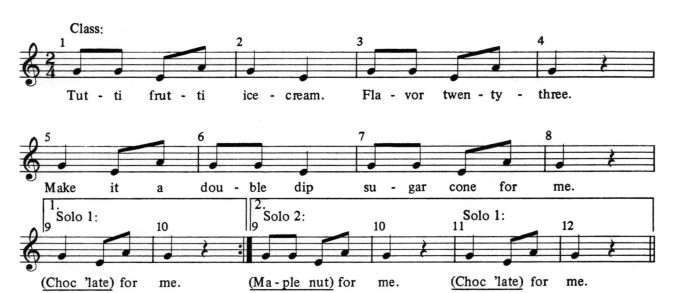

Who Is the Captain?

Pitch content: l,t,drms

Predominant pitch(es)/pattern(s): smrdt,l,   l,m

Suggested grade level(s): 2 and 3

Formation: Circle

Materials required:
- "Who Is the Captain?" page (master 2–90)
- long colored rope or string, with one-foot section of contrasting rope attached
- resonator bells, optional

Preparation:

Make copies or a transparency of the "Who Is the Captain?" page.

Suggested procedure:

Loop and knot the rope, so that it forms a large circle. Class members stand outside the rope circle and hold it with both hands. As the class sings measures 1 through 8, the students pull, hand over hand on the rope, keeping the beat. The class sings the question "Who is the captain now?" The person holding the contrasting section of the rope sings the solo. The class responds with the soloist's name inserted into the last line of the song.

Other ideas:
1. Eliminate the rope and the circle. Play the game from regular seating formation in the class. You designate the soloist who, in turn, selects the next soloist, and so on.
2. Allow the "captain" to play the "Yo Ho" pattern on resonator bells each time it is sung.

180

Who Is the Captain? (2—90)

Class:

1 2 3 4
Yo ho, and pull the an - chor, Yo ho, I'll show you how.

5 6 7 8
Yo ho, and pull the an - chor. Class: Who is the cap - tain now?
Solo: I am the cap - tain now.
(optional)
Class: (Beth) is the cap - tain now.

─────────────────────────── **Who's Next?** ───────────────────────────

Pitch content: t,drmfsltd'

Predominant pitch(es)/pattern(s): drm   drmfs   d'tlslsm

Suggested grade level(s): K to 2

Formation: Teacher's choice

Materials required:

- "Who's Next?" page (master 2–91)
- stickers or other rewards, optional

Preparation:

Make copies or a transparency of the "Who's Next?" page.

Suggested procedure:

Choose a student to sing all three solos, and name him or her as you begin the song. Sing measures 1, 2, 4, 5, 7, and 8. The designated soloist echoes at the appropriate places (measures 3, 6, and 9). The class sings the final four measures, and the soloist is rewarded with a handshake from you.

Other ideas:

1. Designate three different soloists. Each child will sing one solo.
2. Add hand motions to the song:

"Do Re Mi"	(use Curwen hand signs)
"1, 2, 3, 4, 5"	(count fingers on right hand)
"Lalalalalala"	(with both hands, flex fingers while reaching high and wiggling down)

3. Reward each soloist with a sticker (or other reinforcer). Change lyrics to "Good job . . . You deserve a sticker."

182

Who's Next?

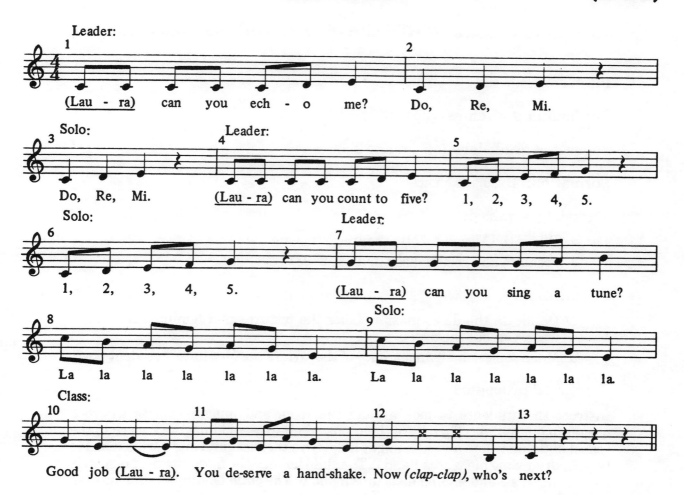

Leader:
(Lau - ra) can you ech - o me? Do, Re, Mi.

Solo:
Do, Re, Mi.

Leader:
(Lau - ra) can you count to five? 1, 2, 3, 4, 5.

Solo:
1, 2, 3, 4, 5.

Leader:
(Lau - ra) can you sing a tune?

La la la la la la la.

Solo:
La la la la la la la.

Class:
Good job (Lau - ra). You de-serve a hand-shake. Now *(clap-clap)*, who's next?

Who's the Mosquito?

Pitch content: ms

Predominant pitch(es)/pattern(s): sm

Suggested grade level(s): preK to 2

Formation: Teacher's choice

Materials required:

- "Who's the Mosquito?" teacher page (master 2–92)
- mosquito and gorilla disks (master 2–93)

Preparation:

1. Duplicate the disks master. Color the pictures and laminate for longer wear. Cut out the disks.
2. Make copies or a transparency of the "Who's the Mosquito?" student page.

Suggested procedure:

Instruct the students to look around the room and imagine places where a mosquito might hide. Then have them close their eyes and imagine a place in the school building where a gorilla might hide. Give the mosquito and gorilla disks to two children. Sing measures 1 and 2. The child holding the mosquito disk responds with measures 3 and 4. Sing measures 5 and 6. The child holding the gorilla disk responds with measures 7 and 8. Instruct the students to give the disks away. Repeat the song.

Other ideas:

1. Have the entire class sing the questions (measures 1, 2, 5, and 6) with you.
2. Seat children in a circle. The whole class sings the questions while passing the disks from child to child around the circle. At measures 3 and 7, the child holding the appropriate disk sings the solo.
3. Use idea #2 in classroom formation.
4. Substitute other animals for the tiny mosquito and large gorilla.

184

Who's the Mosquito?

(2–92)

Leader:
Who's the mos - qui - to and where are you?

Solo:
I'm the mos - qui - to and I'm in the (light switch).

Leader.
Who's the go - ril - la and where are you?

Solo:
I'm the go - ril - la and I'm in the (gym).

(2–93)

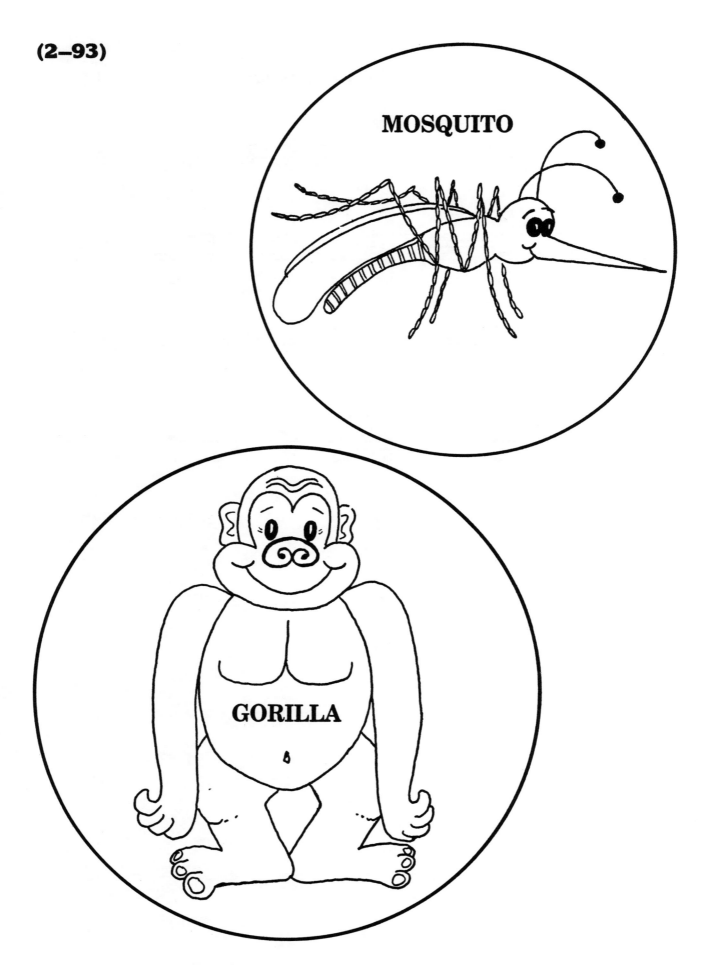

Indexes

Suggested Grade Level Index

Songs Appropriate for Grade Three

Songs Appropriate for Grade Four

Pitch Content Index

Predominant Pitch Pattern Index

196   *INDEXES*

smrdt,l,   **mf#s#l**

Who Is the Captain?, 180   Mister Troll, 144

Subject/Format Index

Name Songs

Question/Response Songs

Social Studies Correlation

Holiday/Calendar Index

Alphabetical Index

CD Track Listing